Strategies in Global Industries

Strategies in Global Industries

How U.S. Businesses Compete

Allen J. Morrison

Foreword by
Hans Schollhammer

Q

QUORUM BOOKS
New York • Westport, Connecticut • London

Library of Congress Cataloging-in-Publication Data

Morrison, Allen J.
Strategies in global industries : how U.S. businesses compete / Allen J. Morrison ; foreword by Hans Schollhammer.
p. cm.
Includes bibliographical references.
ISBN 0–89930–528–8 (lib. bdg. : alk. paper)
1. United States—Commerce. 2. United States—Commercial policy. 3. United States—Industries. 4. United States—Industries–Classification. 5. United States—Foreign economic relations. 6. International trade. 7. Competition, International. 8. Strategic planning—United States. I. Title.
HF3021.M67 1990
338.6′048′0973–dc20 89–24370

British Library Cataloguing in Publication Data is available.

Library of Congress Catalog Card Number: 89–24370
ISBN: 0–89930–528–8

First published in 1990

Quorum Books, 88 Post Road West, Westport, Connecticut 06881
An imprint of Greenwood Publishing Group, Inc.

Printed in the United States of America

The paper used in this book complies with the Permanent Paper Standard issued by the National Information Standards Organization (Z39.48–1984).

10 9 8 7 6 5 4 3 2 1

To my wife Angela,
to my sons Robert and Andrew,
and to my daughter Rachel

CONTENTS

FIGURES

FOREWORD
by Hans Schollhammer

The past few years have witnessed much concern over the competitiveness of U.S. businesses in increasingly global industries. American business has been frequently cited for losing out to the Japanese and West Europeans in areas of quality, costs, and technology. Yet, with these criticisms has also come the growing realization that beyond a limited number of case histories, little is actually known about how U.S. businesses actually compete in global industries.

Strategies in Global Industries: How U.S. Businesses Compete is a study of the content of American business strategies in global industries. Allen Morrison's research, based on an analysis of 115 businesses in 11 different global industries, represents the first attempt to empirically classify the strategies of a broad-based sample of U.S. businesses. As such, this research adds to the knowledge base of both practitioners and researchers interested in understanding the nature and implications of business strategies in global industries.

As chairman of the selection committee for the 1989 Barry M. Richman Best Dissertation Award for the International Management Division of the Academy of Management, it is a pleasure to recommend this book, based on Allen Morrison's award winning dissertation. It presents a comprehensive evaluation and discussion of issues of fundamental concern to those interested in better understanding global competition.

Morrison's study is particularly timely because of the difficulty researchers have had in defining a global industry. The field is replete with conflicting definitions of global competition, often confusing global strategies with global industries. Both mean many things to many people, thus confounding researchers and frustrating efforts by managers to further understand the relationship between environmental imperatives and patterns of strategic behavior. *Strategies in Global Industries* addresses this definitional ambiguity by first controlling for industry "globalness" through a three-stage industry selection process. In all, a set of 11 4-digit SIC code global industries are identified from which his sample of businesses is drawn. It is within this group of classified industries that business strategy content is examined.

One of Morrison's most important contributions is in drawing a clear distinction between a business's internationalization strategy and its competitive positioning. He argues that internationalization—which ranges from global to domestic strategy types—must be considered in combination with a variety of competitive positioning options to determine overall business strategies. Morrison suggests that the two dimensions should be analyzed separately, both for purposes of conceptual clarity and as sources of distinct competitive advantage.

Using this framework, the interaction between competitive positioning and internationalization are identified as four distinct strategy types in global industries. These strategy types include (1) domestic product specialization, (2) exporting high quality offerings, (3) international product innovation, and (4) global combination. Within these strategies, little evidence was available of the low cost of truly global strategies suggested in the literature. Instead, American businesses were found to almost universally emphasize product and service quality based on regional or quasi-international patterns of competition.

After isolating these strategic groups, Morrison then seeks to explain why businesses may pursue different competitive strategies by identifying the perceptions businesses have of industry imperatives. By comparing patterns of strategy behavior to perceptions of competitive pressures, he found extensive mismatches between what businesses perceive to be industry opportunities and how they respond competitively. This was particularly pronounced in the domestic product specialization and exporting high quality offerings groups. The performance implications of poor fit were also explored. Here, it was found that discrepancies between strategy content and perceptions of global industry imperatives led to significant performance differentials; in particular, the domestic and exporting groups showed lower performance levels than the international and global strategy groups.

The broad findings reported in this book suggest that American businesses have generally failed to recognize the extent of environmental opportunities or threats incumbent with industry globalization. Rather, American managers appear preoccupied with domestic competition and perceive U.S. market opportunities as preeminently important. The result is the failure of a broad group of businesses to effective leverage existing international resources to maximize global advantage.

Although Morrison restricts his study to U.S. businesses, the implications of competing in global industries are discussed at length. The book examines three broad themes confronting American managers: (1) the importance which quality offerings play in determining competitive positioning; (2) the nature of the balance between global and regional strategies in defining internationalization; and (3) the influence of global strategic opportunities for U.S. and foreign competitors. These themes suggest that although U.S. businesses appear to be emphasizing many common patterns of strategic behavior, considerable missed opportunities are apparent for American businesses competing in global industries.

In a world in which global competitive pressures are rapidly changing, businesses must become increasingly dependent on accurate and comprehensive assessments of environmental imperatives. While this is true for American businesses, it applies equally well to businesses from developed and developing countries around the world. Clearly, the next step must be to extend Morrison's research to include an examination of business strategies from a variety of home countries. Given the same global industry imperatives, one of the first questions that must be addressed is whether or not home countries bias strategic responses. A more basic question is whether there is a relationship between patterns of strategic response and performance levels which transcend home countries.

Because the marketplaces of the world are becoming ever more integrated, managers and researchers will be drawn increasingly into issues of global competitive analysis. Clearly, Allen Morrison's book provides a major contribution to meeting these challenges that lay ahead.

ACKNOWLEDGMENTS

The development and compilation of the study upon which this book is based were both time-consuming and complex. The encouragement and support of teachers and family members were essential. I wish to gratefully acknowledge their patience and generosity.

I express my deepest appreciation to my Dissertation Committee chairman, Kendall Roth. Professor Roth was a model adviser and chairman who patiently worked with me from the conceptualization of the dissertation through the final draft. His thoroughness, inquiring mind, and painstaking attention to detail are qualities that I shall always strive to emulate. Moreover, the direction he provided goes beyond this study to include a stream of research that will touch upon many of the issues central to the embryonic field of international business strategy.

Professor James Chrisman has had a similarly strong influence on my research and interests in strategic management. He has been particularly influential in encouraging conceptual and theoretical purity in my thinking and has always found time to discuss even the most trivial of concerns. Others contributing to this study included Professor David Ricks, who provided timely comments on my various drafts and was most helpful in providing structure and balance to such a complex project; Professor Douglas Nigh, who encouraged me to synthesize both the domestic and international literature on international business strategy; and Professor

David Schweiger, who was particularly helpful in sharpening my methodological approach and research design.

I would also like to acknowledge the valuable insights into the issues of global competition provided by Professors Brian Toyne and Jeff Arpan. Brian Toyne assisted in further developing my understanding of both the global environment and the theoretical constructs central to international business. Jeff Arpan was most helpful in the early literature review process; he was also instrumental in securing access to essential funding throughout the study. Professors Hans Schollhammer at UCLA, Steve Kobrin at the Wharton School, Don Lessard at MIT, and Nancy Adler at McGill were all influential in providing insightful comments in the early stages of the development of this study. At the University of Western Ontario, I would like to acknowledge the support and encouragement of Professors Mike Geringer and Harold Crookell. Special thanks is also due to Tina Michael for data collection and Penny Sim for typing much of the manuscript.

Finally, I would like to thank my family for the moral and emotional support they provided throughout this research process. I particularly acknowledge my wife Angela for her unwavering support and patience. Without her encouragement, neither this book nor the dissertation upon which it was based would have been attempted. I also recognize the sacrifices of my two young sons, Robert and Andrew, who spent much of their early years wondering why their father seemed to be forever absorbed in his studies. I would also like to thank my parents, who are responsible for instilling in me a desire for excellence and a love of learning.

To these people and others, I owe a great debt of gratitude. To the extent I have been able to address some of the "global" concerns facing businesses in this country, this study will have been a useful endeavor.

Strategies in Global Industries

CHAPTER 1

INTRODUCTION AND OVERVIEW

International trade and competitiveness are issues of critical concern to many businesses today. This is particularly true in America where more frequently than ever businesses are being challenged both at home and abroad in market battles that often threaten the survival of entire domestic industries. With this growing internationalization of competition has come the fear that the competitiveness of a wide variety of business is declining. So pervasive is this concern that in a recent survey of nearly 4,000 American managers 92 percent indicated that U.S. competitiveness was threatened by foreign competitors.[1] In another study, Peters suggested that "fully 70 percent of [U.S.] industries, up from 25 percent only a dozen years ago, are under full-scale attack by foreign competitors."[2]

This internationalization of competition comes at a time when a growing number of industries are facing worldwide homogenization of product demand, extensive economies of scale, and decreasing tariff and nontariff barriers to trade. Increasingly, these highly internationally competitive environments have been characterized as "global industries."[3] The pervasiveness of global industry pressures transcends national boundaries and challenges businesses to alter or revise competitive strategies.[4] In global industries, businesses no longer have the luxury of competing only against domestic firms; rather, rivalries pit American businesses against Japanese businesses, European businesses, and increasingly businesses from newly industrialized countries (NICs) in battles for world market dominance.

Notwithstanding the widespread interest in globalization and the lingering sense that somehow American business is losing the competitiveness war, relatively little is known about the broad strategic patterns of businesses as they relate to global competitive pressures. Practical problems of doing international business research paired with the absence of generally accepted and appropriate theoretical underpinnings have resulted in an abundance of conceptual abstractions. Unfortunately, while unique patterns of American strategic behavior in global industries are implicitly hypothesized in the literature, little empirical support is available to indicate either the content or the importance of these particular patterns.

What patterns of strategic behavior are actually manifested by businesses competing in global industries? This book is designed to address this question through the identification of distinct patterns of strategic behavior by U.S.-based businesses competing in global industries. Furthermore, this book examines the relationship between the patterns of strategic behavior pursued by businesses competing in global industries and respective performance levels. More specifically, the patterns of strategic behavior associated with both superior and suboptimal performance levels of businesses competing in global industries are identified and normative implications discussed. Also discussed is the relationship between patterns of strategic behavior and the environmental pressures that determine industry globalization.

CONCEPTUAL FRAMEWORK

The conceptual foundation for this book is based on an integration of two theoretical perspectives: (1) the contingency perspective of strategic management and (2) the industry organization perspective of the business's context. Together, these two perspectives are vital in furthering an understanding of the relationship between business strategy and performance in global industries. Indeed, implicit in the study of competition in global industries is a recognition of the dominant role that industry context plays as the chief contingency in framing competition. Furthermore, as a unit of analysis for international competition, the global industry has been regarded as most appropriate "because the industry is the arena in which competitive advantage is won or lost."[5]

The basic premise of contingency theory is that there is no single best way to orient the organization and that not all ways of organizing are equally effective under given conditions.[6] With respect to business strategy, contingency theory holds that performance outcomes are determined by matching organizational competencies and abilities with the organization's external context.[7] Indeed, Hofer and Schendel define strategy as "the basic characteristics of the match the organization achieves with its environment."[8] Consequently, what becomes important from a business strategy perspective is the identification of salient contingency relationships.

Industry organization theory suggests that the most critical contingency variable determinant to the organization is the industry setting. The roots of this theory can be traced to the work of Mason and Bain. They argued that a firm's performance was a function of conduct that itself was determined by industry structure.[9] From a strategic management perspective, the unit of analysis shifts from the industry to the business unit, which becomes the focus of competitive analysis.[10] Within an industry context, businesses assess common environmental variance and strategically position themselves according to their particular distinctive competencies. Given particular industry characteristics, business strategy is thus determined after both internal and external assessments are made of firm-specific opportunities and threats.[11] The general framework suggested in the industry organization theory is shown as follows:

INDUSTRY → BUSINESS STRATEGY → PERFORMANCE

Thus, it is suggested by contingency theory that a business must match its strategy and its context, and by industry organization theory that the most important contextual dimension is the industry in which the business competes. The integration of contingency theory and industry organization theory has enabled researchers to identify alternative strategies suggested appropriate for different industry contexts.

Within an industry context, businesses often display dissimilar patterns of "conduct" or business-level strategic behavior in global industries that lead to different levels of performance. By controlling for industry context and comparing different modes of conduct, it is possible to isolate specific patterns of strategic behavior in global industries.

The presence of multiple patterns of strategic behavior in global industries has been widely hypothesized in the literature. For example, Bartlett suggests that global industry pressures encourage competitors to cross-subsidize their international operations in a game that he terms "global chess."[12] Yet how each competitor plays the game varies according to how competitive advantage can best be leveraged. To this end, Porter has asserted that "there is no archetypal global strategy, but numerous ways of competing globally."[13] Prahalad and Doz refer to these different patterns of competition as "strategic intents" that in global industries "lead to very distinct approaches to competition and the use of competitive advantages, even if the strategic infrastructures appear not to be markedly dissimilar."[14]

The identification of a particular pattern of strategic behavior is based on the emphasis businesses place on various strategy variables, where strategy variables are defined as discrete elements of functional-level activities that together determine the business's pattern of strategic behavior. The association of patterns of these variables with differing performance levels can have normative implications for industry members. The suggestion is that businesses desiring to maximize performance should recognize that different patterns of strategic behavior are identified with varying levels of performance. The objective, then, for the business would be to determine which strategy optimized performance.

An important outcome in the identification of patterns of strategic behavior has been the development of classification schemes of business conduct. Researchers have worked at identifying and classifying alternate strategies suggested appropriate for various kinds of industries including, among others, high-growth industries, declining industries, mature industries, and global industries. Fundamental to this work is the ability of researchers not only to classify strategies but also to identify salient industry dimensions on which strategy is contingent.

PROBLEM STATEMENT

Unfortunately, much of the support for the presence of alternate patterns of strategic behavior in global industries is founded on either conceptual arguments or research based on small samples. Essentially no empirical examinations have been made of business-level strategy content in global industries. Exacerbating these shortcomings is the lack of any clear consensus on which strategic components are most critical in a determination of global industry-based business-level strategic behavior. Indeed, few attempts have been made to operationalize business-level strategy in either a broad international context or a more specific global context.

To address these shortcomings, the study presented in this book is directed at responding to the following research questions:

1. Do distinct patterns of strategic behavior exist for businesses that operate within global industries? And if so, what are the dominant elements?

2. Which patterns of strategic behavior are associated with superior performance levels in global industries? Are alternative patterns of strategic behavior equally "effective"?

METHODOLOGY

The design of this study is geared to uncovering strategic patterns through fundamentally an exploratory procedure that is based on and extends prior research. While the foundations of this study are based on integrating conceptual and empirical research in the fields of strategic management, industry organization, and international business, very little is specifically known about how businesses compete in global industries. Consequently, hypotheses that presuppose modes of operation have been viewed as inherently problematic given that confirmatory research requires insights "on which higher order generalizations can be constructed"[15] and that such insights have been lacking in this area of research. Furthermore, the use of empirical methods of classification has been viewed as particularly relevant for emerging disciplines that are "still wrestling with the problems of how best to classify" component objects.[16]

Exploratory research plays a fundamental role in theory development.[17] Beginning with a solid grounding in theory, exploratory research contributes to theory development through empirical generalizations that lead to explanatory and predictive propositions. When propositions of this nature are arranged into a logical deductive system, "the resulting structure is termed a 'theory.' "[18] Only when a theory has been developed can it then be deductively tested for both internal and external validity. This study is limited to the exploratory development of explanatory and predictive propositions that serve as the foundation for international business strategy theory development.

DEVELOPMENT OF THE CLASSIFICATION SCHEME

Six different steps were utilized in developing the classification scheme of business-level strategic behavior in global industries. These steps include:

Step 1: Operationalize global industry and identify industry members
Step 2: Operationalize business-level strategy
Step 3: Derive strategy variables
Step 4: Design and pretest instrument

Step 5: Gather and analyze data
Step 6: Confirm classification through posttest

Each of these steps will now be briefly discussed.

1. *Operationalizing Global Industry and Identifying Industry Members.* Global industries have frequently been discussed in the strategic management literature. Definitionally, global industries have been identified with high levels of cross-border trade flow, high levels of international competition, the worldwide presence of competitors in all key markets, and the worldwide marketing of standardized products by industry competitors.[19]

In order to identify industries meeting this definition of "global," a three-step process was utilized. Step 1, which is discussed in Chapter 2, involved identifying a pool of industries commonly cited in the literature as being global. This pool contained a diverse group of standard industry classification (SIC) code industries identified by a variety of researchers. However, as was found to occur commonly, many of these selected industries were identified as global by researchers who limited their examination to the strategic behavior of a dominant industry competitor. For example, if a company had uniquely established a global distribution network for cosmetics and was found to be globally subsidizing market share battles, the assumption would be made that the entire worldwide cosmetics industry was global. However, as discussed by Bartlett, it is the combination of structural characteristics *and* the combined action of competitors that determine the actual nature of the industry.[20]

Given that industry "globalness" may not be categorical,[21] the second step of the industry selection process involved restricting the sample to only those identified global industries that exhibited high levels of transnational trade in terms of both imports and exports as a percentage of consumption. This step is discussed more fully in Chapter 3. Trade flow levels can be viewed as objective measures of industry exposure to international competitive forces.[22] Here, high trade flow levels are viewed as a necessary but not sufficient condition for industry globalization.

The final step in the industry selection process involved further restricting the sample to industries that would minimize variance across the remaining three key global industry parameters: high levels of international competition, the worldwide presence of competitors in all key markets, and the worldwide marketing of standardized products by industry competitors. The results of this procedure are reported in Chapter 4.

In all, 11 industries were identified as meeting this narrower definition of global. In the selection of businesses competing in the identified industries, only divisional head offices of medium- and large-sized business units or independent businesses were used. A discussion of the sample utilized is found in Chapter 3.

2. *Operationalizing Business-Level Strategy.* A four-dimensional model of business strategy content was developed to assist in the operationalization of business-level strategy. This model, which is discussed in Chapter 2, presents a business's overall strategy as a function of competitive position, investment, political, and integration substrategies. This conceptualization of business strategy represents a broader perspective of possible business activity than has generally been recognized in studies that have predominantly focused on domestic businesses or studies that have not explicitly considered the international dimension of business activity.

Methodologically, this study followed a combination of complementary research processes as widely advocated in the literature.[23] These processes include a reliance on both coarse- and fine-grained methodologies in assessing business strategy, as well as a combination of both primary and secondary data in determining business performance.[24]

3. *Deriving Strategy Variables.*Using the developed four-dimensional model of business strategy content, strategy variables were identified according to the potential competitive position, integration, investment, and political substrategies of business activity in the identified sample. The derivation of the strategy variables is discussed in Chapter 3. Various methodologies including pretest interviews, reviews of existing domestic strategy classification research, and appeals to conceptual international business literature were used in deriving the strategy variables.

4. *Design and Pretest of the Instrument.* As discussed in Chapter 3, a mail questionnaire was used as the principal form of data collection in this study. The questionnaire was subjected to extensive pretesting to ascertain its overall comprehensiveness and objectivity. As a result of the pretesting process, various refinements were made to both the derivation of the strategy variables and the specific wording of questionnaire items.

5. *Data Analysis.* Given the exploratory nature of this study, the data analysis focused on, first, uncovering patterns of strategic behavior and, second, identifying which patterns of strategic behavior yield superior results. To this end, data covering the business units' strategy variables and performance indicators were subjected to various multivariate data reduction procedures, including principal components analysis, cluster analysis, and analysis of variance. The result is the identification of distinct patterns of strategic behavior or strategy "taxa," which are defined as "sets of entities sufficiently similar to each other and sufficiently different from

the entities in other such sets that they are separately delimited and named."[25]

6. *Confirmation of Classification.* Following the preliminary identification of a group of strategy taxa, secondary data sources were employed and follow-up interviews were conducted to verify the accuracy of the strategy classification. Secondary data from 17 different businesses were reviewed, and interviews were conducted with executives from 10 different businesses to assist in the confirmation of the classification. These results are reported in Chapter 4.

CONCLUSIONS

Improving international competitiveness is a fundamental objective of many businesses today. The objective of this study is to identify those patterns of strategic behavior associated with superior performance for U.S. businesses competing in global industries. And while it should be clear that the present inquiry is exploratory, this study represents an important empirical contribution to a growing body of research on global strategy and competition.

By studying competition from a contextual viewpoint it is appreciated that exogenous pressures that encourage particular strategic responses can be perceived differently by businesses within the same industry. Misperceptions of environmental pressures lead to poor strategy-industry fit and missed opportunities for improved performance. Poor strategy-industry fit should be particularly evident in global industries where businesses are buffeted by broad, often incongruent pressures that create ambiguous opportunities and threats. Even after identifying broad patterns of strategic behavior by U.S. businesses, it must be appreciated that strategies pursued by non-U.S. businesses may yet afford opportunities for improved U.S. business performance. This issue is more fully discussed in Chapter 8.

Although this study measures business strategy in global industries, the implications extend beyond this narrow context. The identified classification of business strategies in global industries provides a more complete understanding of how successful businesses compete in the most internationally competitive contexts. By highlighting these patterns of strategic behavior, businesses that do not compete in global industries can nevertheless develop a better understanding of both the pressures of global competition and the means U.S. businesses select to compete in these highly international contexts.

LIMITATIONS ON THE SCOPE OF THIS STUDY

At the outset, it should be noted that this study's scope, while ambitious in many respects, is restricted along several dimensions. The study is limited to uncovering patterns of strategic behavior in American business units; the sample does not include European or Japanese businesses. The sample also omits foreign subsidiaries of U.S.-based companies that may be competing in the same industry as the parent. There are several reasons for this, not the least of which is concern over the manageability of the study. Resource and language constraints, as well as problems of comparability, prohibited a more expansive study.

In support of the U.S. focus of the study, globalization also seems to represent much more of a compelling issue to American managers than to managers in other countries. It seems that American business is only now becoming aware of the great influence global opportunities and threats are having on competitive environments. Undoubtedly much of this preoccupation is the result of heightened concern in the United States over international competitiveness. While conceptually differences in home country status should have little influence on global strategy content,[26] this remains a viable question for future research.

The study also focuses exclusively on the business unit in identifying strategy content. Although the linkage between the global industry context and the business unit is a requisite of the conceptual framework driving the study, it is also recognized that global strategic behavior is not always limited to discrete business units. This is a significant yet unresolved problem confronting both domestic and international strategic management research. The challenge is in balancing needs for comparability of data with the requirements for comprehensiveness and clarity. This is particularly problematic in global industries, given the role the entire organization can play in determining strategy content. To this end, the unit of analysis in this study was framed by its appropriate exogenous industry context, and assessments were made of both internal and external linkages involving the business unit in question. A more complete discussion of the study's limitations is found in Chapter 8.

ORGANIZATION OF THE BOOK

This chapter has presented a brief introduction to the research focus of the study and has provided a review of the methodology to be used in responding to broad research questions. The chapter also provided a justification of the relevance and timeliness of the research undertaken and has discussed limitations on its scope. Chapter 2 reviews the strategic management and international business literature pertinent to research objectives identified in Chapter 1. In particular, corporate- and business-level strategy content is discussed, a four-dimensional model of business strategy is presented, and an identification of global industries and relevant global pressures is made. Chapter 3 discusses in greater detail the methodology used to develop the classification of business strategies in global industries. In Chapter 4, the survey data analysis, secondary data, and posttest interviews are discussed. Four separate strategy taxa are identified in global industries. Chapter 5 relates the identified composite strategies to the international business and strategic management literature. Particular attention is paid to the relationship between internationalization and competitive positioning in determining composite strategies. Chapter 6 explores the relationship between composite strategies and the industry imperative of integration and responsiveness. Performance implications of strategy-industry fit are also discussed. Chapter 7 provides a discussion of the major findings of the study and further addresses three broad themes uncovered through the classification: quality-based competition, the regionalization of competition, and missed strategic opportunities for U.S. businesses. The final chapter of the book presents a discussion of the study's limitations and directions for further research.

NOTES

1. Harvard Business Review (1987:8–11).
2. Peters (1986: 11).
3. Bartlett (1985), Porter (1986a), and Ghoshal (1987).
4. See Ohmae (1985), Cohen and Zysman (1987), Hax (1989), and Hamel and Prahalad (1989).
5. Porter (1986a: 17).
6. For a more complete discussion of the strategic management perspective of contingency theory, see Ginsberg and Vankatraman (1985).
7. See Hofer (1975), Hofer and Schendel (1978), and Ginsberg and Venkatraman (1985).
8. Hofer and Schendel (1978: 4).
9. Mason (1939) and Bain (1968).
10. See Snow and Hambrick (1980), Porter (1981), Harrigan (1983), Ginsberg and Venkatraman (1985), and Dess (1987).
11. See Andrews (1971) and Porter (1981).
12. Bartlett (1985: 10).
13. Porter (1986b: 5).
14. Prahalad and Doz (1987: 52).

15. Bower (1986: 25).

16. Punj and Stewart (1983: 135).

17. Wallace (1971), Schollhammer (1973), Spender (1979), Schendel and Hofer (1979), Sauer, Nighswonger, and Zaltman (1983), and Hambrick (1984).

18. Wallace (1971: 57).

19. See Porter (1980), Cvar (1984), Bartlett and Ghoshal (1987), and Prahalad and Doz (1987).

20. Bartlett (1985).

21. See Porter (1980), Cvar (1984), and Bartlett (1985) for a discussion of the degree of globalization.

22. See Prescott (1983), Cvar (1984), and Porter (1986a).

23. Denzim (1978), Snow and Hambrick (1980), Harrigan (1983), and Venkatraman and Grant (1986).

24. See Harrigan (1983) for a discussion of the merits of course-grained versus fine-grained methodologies.

25. Chrisman, Hofer, and Boulton (1988: 415).

26. Doz (1986) and Porter (1986a).

CHAPTER 2

LITERATURE REVIEW

The purpose of this chapter is to highlight existing research relating to competitive business strategies in global industries. The first section of the chapter reviews the evolution of the current strategic management paradigm. In this section, the hierarchical nature of strategy is discussed and a simple model of strategy content is presented. The second section highlights the theoretical and empirical basis of corporate-level strategic behavior. The chapter then shifts to the third section, which focuses on issues specifically involving business-level strategy. In this section, particular attention is focused on the operationalization and classification of business strategy. The methodology associated with the generation of strategy classifications is also reviewed. The fourth section of the chapter discusses the industry context of international business strategy from a contingency perspective. The fifth section of the chapter presents research questions governing the nature of business strategy in global industries. A brief summary section concludes the chapter.

EVOLUTION OF THE STRATEGIC MANAGEMENT PARADIGM

The earliest contributions to the present strategic management paradigm can probably be traced to C. Barnard's *The Functions of the Executive*, published in 1938. Barnard did much to set the groundwork for those who would follow decades later by defining a complete theory of the organization. It was Barnard who made the initial distinction between organizational effectiveness and efficiency. He also developed the concept of specialization as well as the notion that cooperation was essential to the success and survival of the organization. Although he did not identify it by name, Barnard discussed the concept of strategy formulation, formulation being governed by the executive's conveyance of purpose via determining the ends and means of the organization. Implementation of strategy was also manifested by the role of the executive in developing willingness among the employees.

By the mid-1950s, ideas initiated by Barnard were being refined. Drucker argued that effectiveness was doing the "right" things, that efficiency was doing things "right," and that it is more important to be effective than efficient.[1] Selznick refined Barnard's concept of specialization into the idea of "distinctive competence," which was based largely on the values or character of the organization.[2] And March and Simon introduced the concepts of "bounded rationality" and "dominant coalitions" as refinements of the role and scope of organizational leadership.[3]

In 1962, Chandler addressed the issue of strategy and structure through a historical study of 70 of America's largest corporations. In his study, Chandler traced the growth of firms from simple expansion in volumes of output, to geographic expansion, to vertical integration, and finally to product diversification. As firms grew in complexity, Chandler observed that structure changed from that of a unit firm to a functional organization to a multidivisional firm. From his study, Chandler drew two broad conclusions: (1) structure follows strategy, and (2) firms follow a stagewise developmental sequence for strategies and structures.[4]

By the mid-1960s, more attention was being given to developing appropriate organizational responses to given environmental stimuli. Ansoff, for example, regarded the "strategic problem" as determining how to relate the organization to its environment.[5] Strategy content was focused on (1) product/market scope, (2) a growth vector, (3) competitive advantage, and (4) synergy, which would be achieved both within the organization and between the organization and its environment. Strategy would provide the "rules" that would control all organizational activity. Although these elements of strategy content provided a valuable basis for further development of the strategic management paradigm, definitions were poorly defined and the hierarchical nature of strategy was generally unrecognized.

It was against this background that the strategic management paradigm began to develop more fully. Confusion existed as to what constituted strategy, as well as how strategy related to the various contingencies. It was understood that unless one espoused a pattern of optimal strategies for all businesses,[6] all strategies were themselves contingent.[7] And thus because of this view that strategy is generally firm specific, business policy research tended to focus on general theory and broad, basic studies that concentrated on process rather than on specific, content-oriented topics. Consequently, progress in the paradigm tended to be focused on the development of theories of strategic planning, whereas much less success was seen in the development of theories of corporate and business strategy content.[8]

Also lacking in this stream of literature was basic agreement in terms of the definitional constructs of the paradigm. Even today two major areas of disagreement continue within the field of strategic management. The first dispute, highlighted by Bourgeois, revolves around the issue of whether the formulation of strategy is an incremental (intendedly rational) process or whether it is more accurately characterized as a normative process resulting from a comprehensive evaluation process.[9] Andrews, for example, defines one role of general management as being the "architect of organizational purpose."[10]

A second issue still bubbling with controversy today is whether the origins of strategy are rooted in planned intentions as espoused by strategic managers or simply emergent in the ecologically determined ebb and flow of the organization. This population ecology approach to the study of organizations downplays the role of management in dealing with the forces of natural selection as exerted by a volatile environment.[11] As advocates of this perspective, Astley and Fombrun argue that organizations "can collectively, but not independently, maintain control over their destinies."[12]

These debates continue unresolved. However, regardless of the assumed rationality of the organization or the source of organizational action, by defining strategy as the "pattern" of organizational activity, the researcher is able to rise above much of this debate. Consequently, strategy can be viewed as a phenomenon of organizational activity that may be characterized according to patterns of events independent of human input.[13]

The extent of divergence in the different perspectives of strategy highlights the void and controversy from which the present strategic management paradigm has emerged. According to Schendel and Hoffer:

> The initial strategy paradigm was incomplete in terms of: (1) the nature and clarity of the strategy concept itself; (2) the tasks associated with managing and implementing strategy; and (3) the strategic roles of the general manager.[14]

Defining Strategy

Schendel and Hofer's own approach to strategy is based on a composite definition of strategy built around four separate components: (1) scope, defined in terms of product/market matches and geographic territories; (2) resource deployments and distinctive competencies; (3)competitive advantages of the organization; and (4) synergy or internal fit.[15] These components provide a modest refinement of Ansoff's definition of strategy content.

Noticeably absent from Schendel and Hofer's definition of strategy is the inclusion of goals and objectives. Strategy is regarded as the means to the goals of the organization, and consequently, strategy formulation should necessarily be separated from the goal formulation process. While it is agreed that goal formulation is a process closely tied to strategy formulation, considerable debate remains concerning the determination of organizational goals as a process separate from strategy formulation.[16] To avoid this ends/means debate, Schendel and Hofer argued that the combination of goals, strategy, and policies forms the "grand design" or master strategy for the firm. In this way, they provide a precise conceptualization of a complex concept that they have operationalized in a manner that facilitates related research.

In order to refine Schendel and Hofer's definition of strategy further, an attempt must be made to differentiate between the content of strategy and background factors that contribute to strategy formulation. For example, Schendel and Hofer include distinctive competency as an element of strategy,[17] where, in reality, distinctive competency is an organizational capability that may or may not be utilized in strategy formulation. Similarly, synergy is an objective, or what is hoped a strategy will achieve, not a dimension of strategy content.

Morrison and Roth, building on the strategy components acknowledged by Vancil and Lorange, Hofer and Schendel, Porter, and Bourgeois, suggest that there are actually only two components of strategy: scope and competitive methods.[18] *Scope* is here defined as the "extent of the organization's present and planned interactions with its environment."[19] *Competitive methods* describes the ways organizations seek to apply their skills and resources (distinctive competence) in meeting environmental needs in order best to serve their customers and/or differentiate their products or services from those of their rivals.[20]

Scope and competitive methods collectively define the strategy of the organization. In so doing, it is assumed that both scope and competitive methods are controllable by organizational participants as efforts are made to match the organization's distinctive capabilities/competencies with its competitive environment in pursuit of organizational goals. This "matching" is, in effect, the strategy of the firm.[21] In the match achieved, scope and competitive methods are dimensions of strategy that are difficult, if not impossible, to separate completely.

Contingency Theory

The view that performance outcomes are determined by matching organizational competencies and abilities with a corresponding environmental context represents the contingency perspective of organizational strategy.[22] The basic premise of contingency theory is that there is no single best way to orient the organization but that not all ways of organizing are equally effective under given conditions.[23] Consequently, an organization's overall strategy is contingent on a host of both internal organizational variables and external environmental variables. Organizations that experience common environmental and organizational variables should respond with similar strategies.[24]

The level of organizational-environmental matches has been the subject of considerable discussion.[25] Emerging from this discussion has been the development of functional-, business-, and corporate-level strategies of the organization,[26] which have been viewed as the chief responses to the challenge of matching internal capabilities with external exigencies.[27]

CORPORATE STRATEGY

The notion that strategy is considered to be multidimensional does not have its origins with Schendel and Hofer's 1979 study. In the strategic management field, for example, Hofer's 1975 work proposed a division of strategy where corporate strategy involved selecting industries in which to compete, whereas business strategy was concerned with how best to compete in those industries.[28] Others, including Singer, Tilles, Blau, Andrews, Williamson, and Katz and Kahn, have long recognized the hierarchical nature of the organization through the application of systems theory.[29] For example, Lawrence and Lorsch define differentiation as the "state of segmentation of the organizational system into subsystems, each of which tends to develop particular attributes in relation to the requirements posed by its relevant external environment."[30] The conceptualization of strategy at the systems and subsystems levels is thus a natural outcome of advancements in various fields, including business strategy.

Ansoff was one of the first to highlight the advantages of a multidivisional structure through his consideration of corporate synergies. Although the concept of organizational synergy was not fully pursued at the time, Ansoff proposed various normative statements regarding its applicability as corporate strategy took on a portfolio perspective. He also identified several types of synergy including sales synergy, operating synergy, investment synergy, and management synergy.[31] This same emphasis on corporate-level strategy and organizational synergy was also presented by Tilles, who argued that the most tangible expression of a company's strategy was its allocation of funds and that funds allocation should be decided at the corporate level, not the divisional (business) level.[32]

One of the first authors to provide a normative framework for corporate strategy formulation was R. Katz.[33] Katz developed a set of 12 "rules" of corporate strategy—4 of which are universal in their application and include such principles as always leading from strength and concentrating resources where the company presently has a competitive advantage. He divided the remaining eight principles into three rules for "large" companies (for example, preserving company strengths and stability and giving up trying to get the last dollar of profit out of an item) and five rules for "small" companies (attack when the enemy retreats, be as inconspicuous as possible, and so on). Glueck also identified a list of hypotheses (17 in all) that relate to appropriate business and corporate strategies. Glueck's list includes various external and internal contingencies (such as the state of technological maturity and the dependence of a firm on its competitors), thus making it more comprehensive than the previous work of Katz.[34]

In retrospect, much of this earlier stream of literature can be faulted primarily for its anecdotal propositions or rules and for imbuing the organization with a life dynamic. Far too often the terms of reference are void of specificity (for example, Katz's reference to "large" companies) or are so broadly applicable (Glueck's study suggests that the more dependent the firm is on its competitors, the less offensive it is likely to be in its strategy) as to ring of hollow platitudes. Although the principle of synergy and portfolio strategy were being emphasized, the lack of an empirical data base or conceptual framework severely limited the development of the paradigm.

The importance of business unit interrelatedness as a critical determinant of corporate strategy was largely established by Scott, Wrigley, and Rumelt. This group has led the way in developing useful, replicable operationalizations of corporate-level strategy based on forms of portfolio diversification. Implicit in the approach taken by this group (and others including Stopford and Wells, and Daniels, Pitts, and Tretter) is the linkage between strategy and structure, as initially proposed by Chandler.

Scott's study was based on a sampling of *Fortune* 500 companies in the late 1960s. Later, Child embellished Scott's unpublished model, which proposed a three-stage developmental sequence to describe four stages of organization growth and provided a more substantial link to the growing international focus of organizations. According to Child, these four stages of organizational growth include: (1) single product line with little or no organizational structure; (2) single product line with integrated pattern of transactions and a functional organization structure; (3) multiple product or geographic markets with specialization based on product/market or on geographical area relationships; and (4) multiple product and geographic markets with a grid or matrix based on product/market and geographical relationships.[35]

Scott later reevaluated his conclusions to note that the three steps of company evolution are not small, medium, and large but rather small, integrated, and diversified. He also concluded that the trends toward diversification strategies and divisional structure applied in Europe as well as the United States and that, consequently, the evolution of strategy follows a common pattern internationally.[36]

Wrigley identified single, dominant, related, and unrelated businesses as separate subclass strategies for the stage 3 (diversified) companies from the same Fortune 500 sampling used by Scott. Quoting from Scott, these are:

> (1) *Dominant Business* companies that derive 70–85% of sales from a single business or a vertically integrated chain of businesses;
>
> (2) *Related Business* companies that are diversified related areas, but where no single business accounts for more than 70% of sales;
>
> (3) *Unrelated Business* companies that have diversified without relating new business to old and where no single business accounts for as much as 70% of sales;

(4) *Single Business* where over 95% of sales come from a single product line.[37]

From the data collected in 1967, it was evident that diversified companies tended toward a divisional organization structure.

Rumelt expanded Wrigley's categorical scheme to include a pattern of relatedness among business units within a particular organization. This relatedness scheme was developed in order to reflect each company's unique history and "pattern of relationships among technologies, products, and markets."[38] In his study, Rumelt focused exclusively on relatedness as a function of resource independence.[39] Rumelt's resource-based measures were focused on three separate ratios: (1) the *specialization ratio*, which was measured by the fraction of revenue accounted by for the largest single business unit within the firm; (2) the *related ratio*, which was represented by the fraction of revenues accounted for by a firm's related group of businesses; and (3) the *vertical ratio*, which measured the "proportion of the firm's revenues that arise from all by-products, intermediate products and end products of a vertically integrated sequence of processing activities."[40]

Rumelt's study was attempting to determine the trends in the evolution of the connection between strategy and structure in firms over a 20-year period (1949 to 1969). Some 200 *Fortune* 500 companies were sampled from which Rumelt estimated that the percentage of firms among the *Fortune* 500 having product-division organizations rose from 20.3 to 75.9 during the 20-year period. During the same period of time the percentage of functionally organized firms dropped from 62.2 to 11.2. Rumelt concluded that most of this decrease was due to functionally organized firms adopting product-division organizations rather than simply leaving the top 500 listing. According to Rumelt:

> Combined with a definite positive association between diversification and divisionalization was a secular trend toward divisionalization that affected firms in all strategic categories.[41]

Rumelt also compared diversification strategies with performance. The related diversification strategies, and particularly those employed by related-constrained firms where most component businesses were related, were found to outperform all other strategies, on average. Unrelated conglomerate strategies were found to be the lowest performance, on average.

Stopford and Wells conducted a similar study of the influence of certain organizational characteristics on multinational structure.[42] They based their study on 180 U.S. firms with multinational operations. Stopford and Wells concluded that the degree of diversity abroad, percentage of sales abroad, and amount of reliance on research and development (R&D) were key factors influencing structure.

Daniels, Pitts, and Tretter updated the Stopford and Wells study by examining 93 large U.S. multinationals.[43] They used the same five classifications of organization structure—worldwide functional, worldwide product, international division, area, and matrix structure—employed in the earlier study and product diversity, dependence on foreign operations, strategic emphasis, and ownership and control characteristics as independent measures.[44] The main conclusions in this study mirrored those of Stopford and Wells as well as Rumelt: (1) firms with low to medium diversification strategies tend toward functional organization structures, (2) as business dependence on foreign sales increases there appears to be the major impetus for a shift from a worldwide product to an international division structure, and (3) international divisions that become larger than domestic product divisions tend to be split into two or more geographic areas to provide improved balance in terms of division size. In an effort to summarize the research in this area, Prahalad and Bettis suggest that the linkage between diversity and performance appears to be a function of:

> (1) the generic diversification strategy (governing how much and what kind of relatedness), or
>
> (2) the profit potential of the industries in which individual businesses are positioned and the actual competitive position of the business in each industry, or
>
> (3) the cash flow characteristics of each business, and the cumulative effect of the business units' cash flow within the firm.[45]

In addition, Prahalad and Bettis suggest an elusive "dominant logic" at the corporate level that relates "the strategic variety amongst businesses in the firm, and changes it with the appropriateness of the dominant general management logic(s) that top managers in that firm use."[46] Tregoe and Zimmerman refer to this as the organization's "driving force."[47] The dominant logic or driving force determines the "focus" of the entire organization and consequently its overall performance.

Prahalad and Bettis, and Tregoe and Zimmerman have attempted to highlight a fundamental linkage between a diversification strategy and the overriding orientation of top management. When top management adopts an organizational strategy both internally and externally consistent with the firm's driving force, superior performance can be anticipated. Effective corporate strategy formulation then takes on a human dimension, and although the nature of these managerial skills remains elusive, Prahalad and Bettis in particular argue that strategy is not simply a reflection of organizational structure.

The appropriateness of linking corporate strategy with the structural characteristics of the organization has been the subject of considerable debate. For example, Wrigley, Scott, Rumelt, and others assume that, for the sake of simplicity, organizations can be characterized by one structure and that there are relatively few different structural forms available to management. However, many organizations do not follow predicted courses of development. Bartlett, for example, studied ten such firms and found that behavior changed, whereas structure remained basically constant.[48] Faced with mounting environmental uncertainty, "managers viewed the organizational challenge not as one of finding the right structure but as one of building an appropriate management process."[49] Consequently, much of corporate-level strategy research has focused on issues of portfolio management and managerial process issues. Many of these issues are geared at achieving synergies and balance among business units that subordinate their activities to the interests of the parent corporation.

BUSINESS STRATEGY

Consistent with the previously cited literature, a *business unit* is defined as the divisional organization within a firm that is bounded by a given industry environment.[50] Where the entirety of an organization's activities are contained within a single industry, the corporate level and business level can be regarded as being synonymous.[51] The business unit is also viewed as superscribing the various functional areas within its domain. As previously discussed, the strategic position of the business has two components: (1) the competitive methods of the separate and aggregate of the functional areas and (2) the scope of the present and planned interactions with its environment.[52]

Beyond identifying these two components of a business's strategic behavior, Hofer and Schendel have suggested that strategy formulation be conceptualized around "three different, but related, kinds of substrategies: (1) the competitive position strategies, (2) investment strategies, and (3) political strategies."[53] According to this framework, all three substrategies contain elements of scope and competitive methods that are each emphasized to a different degree. Competitive positioning is distinct from competitive methods in that *competitive positioning* specifies "how the business will relate to the market in which it competes,"[54] whereas *competitive methods* describes the approach used in actually leveraging distinctive competencies. Conceptually, a business determines both the scope of its activities and the competitive methods it will use in formulating competitive positioning, investment, and political substrategies. In determining the overall strategic behavior of the business, Hofer and Schendel argue that typically competitive positioning will dominate investment and political substrategies.

Conceptualizing strategic behavior according to substrategies can facilitate the development of a classification of strategy content. By recognizing substrategies, the researcher can focus on parts of the business's overall strategic behavior, thus providing greater clarity and allowing for a more comprehensive classification. Yet in spite of this utility little consensus exists as to which approaches should be used in measuring overall business-level strategy.

Measuring Business Strategy

In broad terms, there is no generally accepted approach for measuring overall business-level strategy.[55] Nevertheless, research on business-level strategy has typically involved several common methods in operationalizing the construct. Hambrick, for example, suggests four different approaches to strategy measurement that dominate the literature.[56] The first of these approaches is the textural description of strategy. This approach relies principally on case studies in the analysis of business strategies. Case studies are thought of as important teaching tools and useful in the textural operationalization of strategy in theory building. According to Miller and Friesen, a major weakness with the textural approach is that case studies cannot be economically generated and consequently offer little opportunity to generalize across business units. Miller and Friesen, and Snow and Hambrick argue that another problem with the case approach is that the description of strategy can be easily biased according to the researcher's perceptions.[57] Furthermore, case studies do not lend themselves to replication.

Hambrick argues that the second alternative for generalizing business strategy is the measurement of parts of strategies.[58] This approach has focused on one or a few key variables (such as the effects of market share on R&D on profitability) in determining an appropriate strategic posture. Although this approach typically produces relatively reliable measures of the key variables in question, it does not provide a holistic approach to strategy formulation; it fails to capture the breadth of decision areas that define an organization's strategy.[59]

The last two approaches to the study of business-level strategies are conceptually developed typologies (which are based on empirical observation and theoretical development) and inductively derived taxonomies (which are typically developed using multivariate statistical techniques). These two approaches have sprung from a desire to derive empirically and—in the case of conceptually developed typologies—to validate a strategy typology against a backdrop of what has become a proliferation of untested prescriptive typologies.[60]

Classification Schemes. The classification of business strategies has several important advantages. Using classifications brings order and parsimony to a cluttered grouping of related variables. Without a classification scheme, researchers are faced with the challenge of individually dealing with all the variables of interest, each being potentially configured in seemingly endless combinations.[61] Classifications also promote the understanding of broad strategic patterns that can facilitate the development of general guidelines for action.[62] Finally, Wolf suggests that classification must be both the first and the last procedure used in the development of the laws of science.[63] This is echoed by S. Hunt, who suggests that "organizing phenomena often represents the first step in theory development."[64]

According to classification protocol, all classifications are generated by "taxa" or strategy variables that are found in one or more "categories" or strategy constructs.[65] As suggested by Chrisman, Hofer, and Boulton, taxa

> are sets of entities sufficiently similar to each other and sufficiently different from entities in other such sets that they are separately delimited and named. A category is a rank or level in a hierarchical classification which is composed of taxa to which the given rank is assigned.[66]

In the classification of business strategy, a taxon should ideally be operationalized according to subunit or functional-level variables that are controllable by business-level managers.[67] Multiple taxa would be organized in specific strategy categories or constructs, which, according to Hofer and Schendel, correspond with competitive positioning, investment, and political substrategies.[68]

Existing organization classification schemes are generally divided into two groupings: taxonomies and typologies. Most classification scholars refer to empirically derived schemes as taxonomies and conceptually derived approaches as typologies.[69] To McKelvey "the term taxonomy is reserved to apply to the theory of classification and . . . type concepts, which are concepts for arranging phenomena into categories."[70] Taxonomies are developed inductively. Typologies, in contrast, are developed using deductive reasoning. They represent a theorist's attempt to make sense out of nonempirical observations. According to Hambrick, typologies

> have the advantage of often being poetic, that is, they ring true, often sounding very plausible. However, since they are largely the product of rather personal insight, they may not accurately reflect reality.[71]

Chrisman, Hofer, and Boulton suggest that general strategy classifications should be founded on four specific guidelines: (1) the classification should be based on all key strategic characteristics of the entities being classified; (2) classifications should be hierarchical or, in other words, consist of two or more categorical levels; (3) classifications should be timeless or apply equally well to organizations in the past as well as those in the future; and (4) classifications should be parsimonious.[72] A classification that encompasses these attributes should achieve a high degree of effectiveness based on the objectives of the scheme.

The initial application of strategy typologies to business units is largely credited to Hofer.[73] Hofer, drawing on the earlier work of Levitt, espoused the product life cycle concept by arguing that "the most fundamental variable in determining an appropriate business strategy is the stage of the product life cycle."[74] Additional pioneering work in this area can be attributed to Miller and Friesen who combined a case review of 81 businesses with a Q-type factor analysis to develop ten archetypes of business strategy.[75] Although their work was admittedly preliminary and their sample base somewhat unorthodox, Miller and Friesen encouraged a trend toward the development and empirical testing of business strategy typologies.

A review will now be made of both the deductively derived typology and the inductively derived taxonomy approaches to strategy classification, with a goal of identifying how scope, competitive methods, and performance of organizations have been operationalized in a domestic context. Another goal of this review is to highlight the methodology employed in the development of domestic classification schemes, with an aim of applying this same methodological approach in a global setting.

Deductively Derived Typologies

Perhaps the best known conceptually derived typology is that presented by Porter. Porter's three generic strategies are based on the profitability of the firm and include cost leadership, differentiation, and focus strategy. According to Porter:

> Effectively implementing any of these generic strategies usually requires total commitment and supporting organizational arrangements that are diluted if there is more than one primary target. . . . [These] generic strategies are approaches to outperforming competitors in the industry.[76]

Furthermore, Porter argues that "the firm failing to develop its strategy in at least one of the directions—a firm struck in the middle—is in an extremely poor position" and is doomed to essentially low profitability.[77]

Porter's generic strategies are based on the competitive methods and scope of the organization, both of which compromise its strategy. His recommendations have intuitive appeal. Unfortunately, Porter does not cite any contributing literature in the development of his typology. It is also unfortunate that Porter's deductively derived typology was not accompanied by an attempt to validate its contents empirically. However, separate research efforts have been directed at subjecting Porter's conceptualized typology to empirical verification. A review of several of these studies indicates mixed results in confirming Porter's typology.

One of the first empirical tests of Porter's hypothesis was conducted by Dess and Davis, who examined 22 firms in the paint and allied products industry.[78] A total of 78 executives from these firms completed questionnaires by indicating the importance of 21 competitive variables.[79] The resulting correlation matrix of these characteristics was subjected to factor analysis to isolate the competitive dimensions associated with Porter's three generic strategies. The principal factor solution retained three elements that were matched against Porter's generic strategies. A panel of seven academicians was then surveyed to determine the importance of each competitive method for each of the generic strategies. Overall, general agreement was achieved between the panel's definition of cost leadership and differentiation and that derived via the factor analysis. However, disagreement existed over the panel's notion of focus strategy and that which was labeled through the derivation.

In order to differentiate firms according to distinct patterns of strategic behavior, Dess and Davis entered the factor scores of each firm into a cluster algorithm. Performance data (return on assets and annual sales growth) were provided for 15 of these firms. The authors observed four separate clusters, of which three were regarded as pursuing distinct generic strategies (cost leadership, differentiation, or focus). They labeled the fourth cluster "stuck in the middle." Return on assets for both the cost leadership and differentiation strategies were significantly higher than that generated by the "stuck in the middle" strategy, lending some support to Porter's contention that generic strategies produce superior performance. However, the focus cluster was also shown to have the lowest profitability, indicating that Dess and Davis's results were not conclusive. The authors also raised questions about interpretation of factor scores, given concerns they had with the stability of factor loading in the sample set. The study is also limited in that it involved only one industry.

In a separate study, White examined 69 business units from 12 different businesses from the Profit Impact of Marketing Strategies (PIMS) data base in order to determine the "proper" organizational requirements prescribed for Porter's three generic strategies.[80] A differentiation strategy was operationalized by high relative cost and price, whereas a cost leadership strategy was defined by low relative price and cost. The organizational "context" of the business unit was operationalized along three dimensions: autonomy, frequency of reports/reviews, and functional coordination. Performance was determined according to return on investment (ROI), real sales growth, relative market share, and cash flow from investment.

By statistically comparing different organizational characteristics, White was able to demonstrate that businesses within a common strategy class had similar organizational contexts within the overall corporation. For businesses that pursued a cost leadership strategy, higher ROIs were associated with low autonomy and more frequent reviews and measures of performance. For businesses following differentiation strategies, higher ROIs were associated with an opposite set of interorganizational characteristics. These results were consistent with Porter's contention.[81] However, when White employed other measures of performance (for example, real sales growth), the previously mentioned relationships did not always hold. In addition, the combination strategy of both low cost and differentiation produced the highest overall ROI results and higher real growth results than a simple pure cost strategy. This suggests that, contrary to Porter's hypothesis, some successful businesses follow a combination of two or more "generic" strategies simultaneously.

Another study based on testing Porter's hypothesis was performed by Woo and Cool.[82] The primary ambition of this study was to contrast the performance of Porter's differentiation and cost leadership strategies with nongeneric strategies. The study concentrated on domestic manufacturing businesses over the period from 1976 to 1979 and used the PIMS data base. Woo and Cool chose relative price and cost as representative of the major dimensions that reflect Porter's differentiation and cost leadership strategies. Performance was represented by four factors: return on investment, real sales growth, relative market share, and cash flow to investment. An analysis of variance (ANOVA) procedure was performed that indicated mixed results for the generic strategies. According to Woo and Cool, "In all cases, non-generic strategies as a group seem to perform as well as the generic strategies."[83] These results seem to confirm those findings of White. In addition, the use of discriminant analysis identified differences in the functional components of Porter's two generic strategies and revealed that (1) differentiation strategy was identified with higher product quality and product R&D and (2) cost leadership was associated with lower discretionary spending and a heavy emphasis on forward integration. In all, Woo and Cool's conclusions challenged two aspects of Porter's hypothesis, namely, that generic strategies produce superior performance and that the functional components of particular generic strategies are static and deductively identifiable.

Inductively Derived Taxonomies

A major frustration voiced by those attempting to validate Porter's generic strategies empirically is that the specifics of marketing strategy, funds allocation, the direction of R&D, and so on, are lacking in the original typology. In response to these and other previously mentioned limitations and constraints of the deductively derived typologies, attempts have been made to derive inductively taxonomies that do not begin with an assumed strategic pattern. The taxonomic approach has been viewed as a "state-of-the-art" approach for studying business-level strategy.[84]

Efforts have been made to derive empirically the pattern of strategic behavior of the firm through what has typically been a three-stage process: (1) strategic variables are operationalized; (2) through the use of questionnaires, variables are subjected to factor analytic tests; and (3) cluster analysis is performed to identify common groups of strategic patterns. Four separate attempts to generate inductively derived taxonomies will now be examined.

C. Galbraith and Schendel conducted one of the most ambitious attempts to derive a business strategy typology statistically.[85] Using the PIMS data base, Galbraith and Schendel were able to access detailed business-level and time-series information on 1,200 consumer goods and industrial products businesses. They identified a total of 26 managerially controlled variables, 13 of which represented the relative strategic posture of the businesses with respect to their competitors, whereas the remaining variables reflected changes in strategy over time. From these 26 variables, the methodological approach utilizing both principal components analysis and cluster analysis identified six strategy types for consumer products: harvest, builder, cashout, niche or specialization, climber, and continuity. The study also identified four strategy types for industrial products businesses: low commitment, growth, maintenance, and niche or specialization. Galbraith and Schendel then computed the impact of these strategy types on performance, according to three measures of performance: mean values for cash flow, return on investment, and percentage annual change in market share position.

In raising questions about the validity of their classification, Galbraith and Schendel, at the outset of their study, stated their concern over how the variables in the PIMS data base were operationalized. Specific concern was also expressed over the pooling of cross-section and time-series data, and the multicollinearity of variables.[86] Clearly, a major problem with using PIMS data is the lack of direct measures of strategic behavior. Chrisman, Hofer, and Boulton also fault Galbraith and Schendel for the conceptual approach the authors took: by segregating industrial goods from consumer goods manufacturers, they developed two separate strategy typologies.[87] Instead of developing a "true" general classification, Galbraith and Schendel's set was sample specific and nonexhaustive. Thus, while it is a seminal taxonomic contribution, Galbraith and Schendel do not provide a holistic taxonomy of strategy types.

Using a similar methodology, Robinson and Pearce attempted to derive statistically a set of generic strategies through a study of 97 small North Carolina manufacturing firms.[88] These firms represented six different manufacturing industries.[89] Robinson and Pearce obtained responses of chief executive officers (CEOs) to determine the degree to which their firms used 22 different competitive methods over the last five years. The authors based the design of the set of competitive methods on the input of industry consultants, previous conceptually derived typologies, and questionnaire items used in previous research.[90] Elements of performance measured included return on assets, sales growth, and return on sales.

Using factor analysis, Robinson and Pearce identified four distinct strategic factors: efficiency, service, product innovation and development, and brand and channel influence. They tentatively viewed these factors as generic in that the factors were repetitive across the numerous industries in the sample. Robinson and Pearce then performed a cluster analysis in order to separate firms into strategic groups. The cluster analysis suggested that instead of emphasizing only one pattern of strategic behavior, firms appeared to emphasize multiple combinations of the generic strategies. Overall, five strategic groupings became evident. When these groupings were compared with performance levels, several patterns were apparent. Two groupings of strategic behavior (either the combination of "brand identification/channel influence" and "efficiency" or a primary emphasis on "product innovation/specialty" with a secondary emphasis on "service/high price") seemed to provide firms with significantly higher performance than firms that showed no clear strategic direction or firms that had only a marginal emphasis on "brand/channel influence" and "service."

In another taxonomic study, Davis used a secondary data source developed by the Center for Industry Policy and Strategy (CIPS) at the University of South Carolina.[91] The CIPS data base includes responses from 363 strategic business units competing in the paper products industries, representing six different SIC codes. Davis restricted his study to two of the industries that represented almost 80 percent of the business units in the data base. Business-level strategic behavior was operationalized by drawing on the contributions of both Porter, and Dess and Davis and involving executive evaluations of the importance of 30 different strategic variables.[92] Performance was measured by total sales growth and after-tax return of total assets.

Through the use of factor analysis of the executives' responses, Davis identified six strategic factors: (1) production efficiency, (2) differentiation, (3) specialty production, (4) research leadership, (5) geographic concentration, and (6) cost consciousness. The appropriate factor scores were then inputted into a cluster analysis to determine patterns of strategic behavior. Ten clusters were identified, and of these, Davis concluded that a strong emphasis on both low price (that is, cost efficiency) and marketing and distribution (product differentiation) provided the highest overall performances. In contrast, the study identified strategic patterns that resulted in the lowest overall performances as those businesses that emphasized multiple approaches to competition in a limited geographic market ("schizophrenics") and those businesses that emphasized specialty products, also within a limited geographic market ("antiquated traditionists"). Not surprisingly, the next two worst-performing combination strategies both contained elements of geographic "myopia" on the part of businesses that were uninterested in expanding into new markets.

The last inductively derived taxonomy to be reviewed was developed by Roth.[93] Roth also used the CIPS data base. The purpose of this study was to determine the nature of the dual imperative demands of internationalization—one imperative demanding increased effectiveness in the light of a new environmental context and the other requiring increased organizational efficiency to remain cost competitive—as they related to domestically generated combination generic strategies. The hypothesized generic strategies included low cost/efficiency, brand and distribution, product specialization, and service. In addition, Roth wanted to determine the effect of corporate interrelatedness on the pursuance of combination strategies at the business level. The rationale behind this would be that "sharing across business units establishes differentiation capacity through increasing the uniqueness of the differentiating value activity or lowering the cost of the activity."[94] Roth determined business unit performance as a function of three factors: (1) an antecedent strategy of internationalization; (2) some combination of generic strategies; and (3) corporate strategy based on interrelatedness. Performance was determined as a function of comparative sales growth, after-tax return on sales, and after-tax return on assets.

Using a linear structural relations (LISREL) program, Roth attempted to confirm the hypothesized causal structures through the covariance matrix previously established. Thirteen strategic variables were isolated from the original 30 in the data base. Two samples were separated from the large CIPS data base, with one being used as a reconfirmation of the model established by the first. From this procedure, Roth established the presence of three of the four hypothesized generic strategies: low cost/efficiency, brand and distribution, and product specialization. He also concluded that whereas greater corporate interrelatedness is directly associated with a higher emphasis on a combination strategy of (1) low cost/efficiency and distribution and (2) low cost/efficiency and product specialization, no such relationships were established with regard to an antecedent internationalization strategy. Independent of the antecedent strategies, Roth found that "a business unit's pursuit of a combination strategy is not related to superior economic performance."[95] In summary, Roth determined the existence of three generic strategies, he established that a corporate interrelatedness strategy was significantly more influential in encouraging business units to adopt combination strategies than was the case for an antecedent internationalization strategy, and he concluded that combination strategies did not produce superior economic performance.

Summary of the Strategy Classification Approaches

A total of seven studies have been reviewed that attempt to either confirm or establish a classification of business strategies. Three of these studies were aimed at deductively deriving a typology in response to Porter's (1980) three generic strategies; the other four were geared at inductively developing a taxonomy of business strategy. The approach used in each study indicates a predisposition toward the existence of generic strategies. Although each study concluded with the categorization of patterns of strategic behavior, little agreement exists over the common elements among them. What this review has attempted to highlight is not the divergence of conclusions but a commonality of both methodology and the operationalization of business-level strategy in order to identify salient strategy taxa. The methodology associated with these studies is reviewed in Figure 2.1.

The operationalization of the strategy variables in the cited studies was either self-generated or based on previous operationalizations in other studies or was some combination of the two. In Figure 2.1, an effort has been made to include only those strategy variables deemed to explain a "significant" portion of the variance associated with possible strategic behavior. In so doing, it is understood that there are clear difficulties inherent in comparing factor loadings across data bases. This problem is exacerbated when different data analysis techniques (such as factor analysis and principal components analysis) have been used to achieve similar objectives. Consequently, the determination "significant" amount of variance has been largely deferred to the particular authors of each study. For example, Robinson and Pearce identify 16 of their original 22 competitive methods as exhibiting factor loadings greater than or equal to 0.46, which is the cutoff these authors use.[96] In the case of Dess and Davis, factors were considered discriminating with loadings of at least 0.4.[97]

By comparing the overall elements of strategy in the seven studies reviewed, it is possible to isolate 17 strategy variables that are identified in two or more studies as discriminating strategic behavior. Interestingly,

Figure 2.1
Strategy Classification Research Methodology

STUDY	DATA ANALYSIS APPROACH	MEASURE OF PERFORMANCE	NUMBER OF VARIABLES*
Galbraith and Schendel (1983)	-principal components analysis -cluster analysis	-cash flow -ROI -percentage of annual change in market share	26/17
Robinson and Pearce (1985)	-factor analysis -cluster analysis	-ROA -sales growth -return on sales	22/16
Roth (1986)	-LISREL	-comparative sales growth	13
Davis (1986)	-factor analysis -cluster analysis	-sales growth -ROA	30/27
Dess and Davis (1984)	-factor analysis -cluster analysis	-sales growth -ROA	21/16
White (1986)	-principal components analysis	-ROI -sales growth -relative market share -cash flow on investment	2
Woo and Cool (1983)	-ANOVA -discriminant analysis	-ROI -sales growth -relative market share -cash flow on investment	2

* numerator represents original number of variables; denominator represents those variables with high relative loadings

Figure 2.2
Competitive Position Substrategy Variables

HIGH VARIABLE LOADINGS	Galbraith and Schendel (1983)	Robinson and Pearce (1985)	Dess and Davis (1984)	Davis (1986)	Roth (1986)
Emphasize product quality	X	X	X	X	X
Promote new product development	X	X	X	X	X
Build brand identification		X	X	X	X
Emphasize specialty products		X	X	X	X
Develop innovative marketing techniques		X	X	X	X
Emphasize customer service/ service quality	X	X	X	X	X
Develop efficient manufacturing process			X	X	X
Utilize skilled labor		X	X	X	X
Influence/control channels of distribution		X	X	X	X
Price below competitors		X		X	X
Produce products in high priced market segments		X	X	X	
Emphasize plant newness	X			X	
Tightly control overhead and variable costs				X	X
Promote innovation in manufacturing process	X	X	X	X	X
Build reputation in industry		X	X		
Emphasize advertising/ promotion	X		X	X	
Forecast/track market opportunities constantly			X	X	

these variables can all be considered as elements of competitive positioning and are found in Figure 2.2.

Remaining unspecified in Figure 2.2 are the particular strategic variables associated with each of the other two substrategy dimensions posited by Hofer and Schendel.[98] While the deductive and inductive classification studies reviewed utilized variables associated with political and investment substrategy constructs, in only a few instances were variables associated with these substrategies found to discriminate business strategy in the representative samples.

The preeminence of competitive positioning substrategy variables is consistent with the predictions of Hofer and Schendel.[99] Yet to some extent this may be more a reflection of the samples utilized than the universal dominance of competitive positioning itself. Although the samples used in each of the seven studies reviewed contained domestic and multinational business organizations, no attempts were made to capture the essence of competing across multiple national markets. Consequently, to the extent that competitive position substrategies are directed at orienting the business in a given competitive environment, it would be expected that the essence of competing across multiple political and economic environments has not been fully captured in the reviewed studies. While competitive positioning has been shown to play a dominant role in determining strategy content in a domestic context, political and investment substrategies should not be categorically dismissed as elements of strategic behavior in global industries. Indeed, it can be anticipated through contingency theory that patterns of substrategy emphasis will vary extensively according to industry context.

THE GLOBAL INDUSTRY CONTEXT OF BUSINESS STRATEGY

The identification of salient components of business-level strategy is a necessary prerequisite to uncovering patterns of strategic behavior through a contingency perspective of organizational strategy. As discussed in Chapter 1, "contingency theories state that the appropriateness of different strategies depends on the competitive settings of business."[100] Here the industry has frequently been regarded as the basis of competition for the firm.[101] Indeed, according to Christensen:

> The aspect of the environment that most tangibly affects a company is the competitive environment of the industry or industries in which it does business. In each of its businesses, the company faces an

industry structure that shapes the rules of competition it must respond to or try to influence and motivates the attempt to develop an innovatively unique strategy.[102]

Identifying Global Industries

As has been done with business strategies, industries have been the subject of various classification attempts. The advantage of classifying industries is that it enables the isolation of "relatively homogenous environments in which to examine competitive strategies."[103] Perhaps the most noted industry classification scheme is found in Porter who suggests five generic industry environments as the basis of business competition: emerging, mature, declining, fragmented, and global.[104]

The identification of global industries has been the subject of considerable research. Unfortunately, much ambiguity exists over what a "global" industry actually means.[105] Most of this confusion stems from inconsistency in applying industry dimensions in defining industry contexts. For example, Hout, Porter, and Rudden, and Hamel and Prahalad both defined global industries according to a business strategy where competitive position in one national market is subsidized by competition in other national markets.[106]

Such an approach to industry identification has been common in studies of competition in global industries. It is, however, inconsistent with the need to define the industry context independent of strategy. This pattern has been set in studies developing business strategy classifications in other generic industries. For example, Dess as well as Keels et al. have identified a variety of common strategies in fragmented industries but only after first identifying and controlling for industry context.[107] Similar approaches were followed by Zeithaml and Fry, Hambrick and Scheter, and Harrigan, who researched strategies in mature industries; by Aaker and Day, and Yip, who examined strategies in emerging industries; and by Harrigan, who also identified strategies in declining industries.[108]

Beyond identifying global industries through dominant patterns of business strategy, four key structural dimensions have consistently been cited as fundamental to independently defining global industries. First, global industries have been associated with *intense levels of international competition.*[109] This intense competition is encouraged by the globalization of markets, which is represented by the worldwide standardization of buyer demand.[110] From a structural perspective, global industries have been characterized by the dominance of *competitors marketing a stan-*

darized product worldwide.[111] As a result of intense international competition and the marketing of standardized products worldwide, global industries have also been identified by the presence of *industry competitors that have a presence in all key international markets.*[112] Finally, global industries have been differentiated by *high levels of international trade* in terms of product flow across national borders.[113] Indeed, according to Cvar, a necessary condition of industry globalization is the "cross-border flow of a significant portion of components that make up the total cost of the product."[114]

Using these broad dimensions of global industries, various attempts have been made to identify and discuss the structural dynamics of specific global industries. In examining patterns of global production, Flaherty, for example, isolated five U.S. industries at the two-digit SIC code level that displayed significant patterns of globalization: chemicals (SIC 28), nonelectrical (SIC 35), electrical (SIC 36), transport (SIC 37), and instruments (SIC 38).[115]

Further attempts to refine this conceptualization of global industries from two-digit SIC code levels to three- and four-digit SIC code levels have been relatively common. This work includes the identification of the following as global industries: civil aircraft (including engines and parts), watches and watch parts, automobiles, tires, semiconductors and computer devices, sewing machines/textile machinery, heavy machinery/crushing equipment, medical diagnostic equipment, pharmaceuticals/agrochemicals, oilfield machinery and equipment, and household audio and video equipment.[116]

In reviewing this list of identified global industries, several points should be made. First, the individual researchers generally did not attempt to be exhaustive in their individual identifications of global industries. Second, most of the identified industries were selected through an individual case study, often conducted by a single researcher. These studies would then be cited time and again by a core group of global strategy researchers, who would by their citations add credence and credibility to the original classification. In addition, many of these same industries were initially selected because of evidence that individual businesses were competing globally and not that a particular industry had specific global characteristics. For example, the strategies of Caterpillar and Komatsu discussed by Hout, Porter, and Rudden are used to indicate globalization in the entire construction and heavy equipment industries by Doz.[117] Third, there is little consistency in considering industries at a particular SIC code level. For example, Cvar identifies crushing equipment, which is a member of the larger, four-digit SIC code mining machinery industry.[118] Similarly, chemicals (two-digit SIC code) and semiconductors (four-digit SIC code) are discussed as representative of the same level of abstraction in identifying global industries. Indeed, there are a host of different chemical industries—including agricultural wholesale products, industrial wholesale products, photographic compounds, catalysts, and medicinal products—that are contained within the two-digit SIC code industry. Clearly, some may and some may not be global.

Much of the inconsistency in identifying global industries can be traced to the inability of researchers to quantify or compare objectively industries according to levels of emphasis on specific industry structural dimensions. Relatively little attention is paid to actual industry characteristics. Strategies are used to define industries. Levels of trade and international competition, the marketing of standardized product worldwide, and the presence of competitors in all key international markets are cited as critical definitional variables and yet are frequently ignored in identifying global industries. Much of the reason for this is "that 'globalness' is inevitably a matter of degree," and the degree to which an industry is global is viewed as shifting with time.[119] The evolution of an industry into a global state is due to changing environmental factors and strategic repositioning on the part of industry competitors.[120]

The Importance of International Trade Flow Levels. Recent empirical investigations by both Prescott and Cvar have identified international trade flow levels as a necessary dimension in determining the globalness of industries.[121] Unlike the more anecdotal casework of their colleagues, both Prescott and Cvar used quantifiable measures of transnational trade flows in identifying global industries.[122] These studies have indicated that, at very high levels, exports and imports become the most salient single variables in classifying industries. As a consequence, trade flow can be seen as an important instrument in determining the extent of globalization within a given industry. In addressing this issue, Porter has suggested that

> intra-industry trade is a good sign of the presence of global competition, and its growth is one indication that the incidence of global industries has increased.[123]

Prescott's research in this area is based on the PIMS data base with which he classified 311 businesses using 17 different environmental variables.[124] In the identification of eight generic industry classifications, Prescott concluded that two industries—global importing and global exporting—could be characterized solely according to industry import and export levels.[125] Cvar, in her study of competition in 12 industries, pooled export and import flows and classified global industries where "the total imports and exports of product in each major market area of the world were approximately 55 percent of total industry product."[126] Through these industry classifications, both Prescott and Cvar were able to isolate unique patterns of strategic behavior in their identified samples.[127] Parenthetically, it is important to note that a necessary (but not sufficient) minimum trade flow level requirement of only 30 percent—identified by Prescott—would disqualify several frequently cited industries as not adequately meeting the definition of global.

BUSINESS STRATEGIES IN GLOBAL INDUSTRIES

Although considerable attention has been focused on global industry–based competition, systematic research of business strategy content in global industries has been limited. Applicable research has primarily stressed the identification of the broadest patterns of strategy content through selected case studies. These case studies have focused primarily on the geographic aspects of product-market scope in identifying taxa. Typical of this work is that of Porter, who suggests that four competitive strategies dominate competition in global industries: broad line global competition, global focus, national focus, and protected niche.[128] A similar classification is presented by Leontiades, who also suggests the viability of four distinct competitive strategies: global high market share, global niche, national high market share, and national niche.[129] Other classifications abound; unfortunately, researchers are left wondering about the objectivity, comprehensiveness, and consistency of the characteristics used to generate these taxa.

Existing classifications of business strategy in global industries typically focus on two distinct categories of strategies: global and nonglobal strategies. Global strategies are based on globally leveraging distinctive competencies in the cross-subsidization of national market share battles.[130] Unfortunately, the ambiguity of this classification of strategies leaves indeterminate a variety of important attributes. For example, a global strategy could be used to describe a business that locates all of its value activities in its home market and competes on the basis of differentiation; alternatively, it could be used to describe a business that internationally positions and integrates its activities in the pursuit of low-cost competitive positioning.

In contrast, nonglobal strategies can be pursued under a variety of contexts. This category of strategies typically includes variations of domestic, multidomestic, and transnational responses to the imperative of globalization.[131] The major weakness with this category of nonglobal strategies is again its lack of specificity. For example, little is known about the types of domestic strategies that may be most effective in a global context. Indeed, as has been extensively shown in the strategic management literature, domestic strategy content varies considerably in terms of cost and differentiation.

A Broader Conceptualization of Business Strategy

Little has been done to expand these case-based or conceptually generated classifications through a more rigorous examination that incorporates improved methodologies and a broader conceptual foundation. The previously reported review of taxonomies and typologies in nonglobal contexts suggests that competitive positioning plays an essential role in differentiating business strategies. Unfortunately, little has been done to account for competitive positioning in generating existing case-based global strategy classifications.

Case-based global industry strategy classification schemes are also restricted by focusing on only the geographic dimensions of product-market scope. Businesses competing internationally operate in multiple, broadly divergent national contexts. This in turn suggests exposure to a diverse set of cultural and political contexts that add complexity to the requisite strategic responses of businesses. Competitive positioning alone is insufficient in assisting businesses in their interactions with this broader set of factors.[132]

Given the added importance that cultural and political environments play in global industries, researchers have posited the existence of further substrategy dimensions beyond competitive positioning identified in the previously noted classification research. These include political and investment substrategies suggested and previously discussed by Hofer and Schendel[133] and an integration substrategy suggested by A. Morrison and Roth.[134]

Although in a domestic context the utility of employing a broader framework of business strategy has been largely viewed as nondiscriminating, in an international context investment, political, and integration substrategies have been posited as providing a fundamental expansion of the conceptualization of business strategy.[135] This is supported by Chrisman, Hofer, and Boulton who contend that the relative importance of substrategies varies according to critical contingencies.[136] A brief discussion of these three additional substrategies follows.

Political Substrategies. Although potentially all businesses are affected by their respective political environments, businesses with global operations are particularly susceptible to a variety of political pressures. On a conceptual basis, political strategies tend to be directed toward either identifying attractive national markets or winning host nation concessions. The aim of a political strategy is to obtain and sustain a competitive advantage from noneconomic actors, including the government, the general public, special interest groups, and so on.[137] Commenting on Porter's three generic strategies, Boddewyn has argued that "if a firm cannot be a cost, differentiation or focus leader, it may still beat the competition on another ground, namely, the non-market [political] environment."[138]

Successfully operating within multiple national political environments requires the identification of rules by which particular political tactics may be employed under diverse conditions.[139] Four overriding "rules" that govern hands-on political activity continue to be emphasized in the literature. These include: (1) using international political risk forecasting, (2) using political skills to lobby for favorable host nation government policies (e.g., reductions in local content, offset provisions), (3) safeguarding local operations from host nation intervention, and (4) securing the assistance of the U.S. government or governmental agencies in penetrating foreign markets. Variables associated with political substrategies are shown in Figure 2.3.

Integration Substrategies. Integration substrategies can be designed to link either discrete activities within the firm or between firms. While internal and external integration substrategies both strive to capitalize on the firm's distinctive competencies, there are fundamental differences in how they go about "matching" the firm to its environment. Internal integration substrategies are based primarily on exploiting host nation market disequilibria through internalization advantages. External integration substrategies are fundamentally designed to increase the business's scope of activity, also largely through the advantages of internalization.

Internal Integration: The Role of Internalization. Internal integration takes place across functional units within the business unit. Kogut and Porter have suggested the value-added chain as representative of the generic functional activities specific to the business unit.[140] Porter separates these activities into five "primary" and four "support" functions that identify the firm. Primary activities include inbound logistics, operations,

Figure 2.3
International Political Substrategy Variables

VARIABLES	STUDIES
Use international political risk forecasting	Kobrin (1982); Simon (1982); Poynter (1983); Moran (1985); Boddewyn (1986); Sethi and Luther (1986)
Use political skills to lobby for favorable host government policies (e.g., offsets, % local content)	Benson (1975); Tomlinson (1980); Blake (1981); Moran (1985); Boddewyn (1986); Doz (1986); Pfeffer (1987)
Safeguard local operations from host nation intervention	Fagre and Wells (1982); Poynter (1983); Kogut (1985b); Doz (1986); Encarnation and Wells (1986); Porter and Fuller (1986)
Secure assistance of U.S. government/agencies in penetrating foreign markets	Rabino (1980); Czinkota and Ricks (1981); Czinkota (1982); Hafbauer and Erb (1984); Caves and Jones (1985)

outbound logistics, marketing and sales, and service. Support activities represent the infrastructure of the firm, its technical development capacity, procurement, and human resource management. Value chains are specifically controlled by the business unit, with the geographic location of individual components of the value chain determined by factors dictated by host nation environments and the industry context. However, to the extent that make or buy decisions, information exchanges (including technology), trade arrangements, funding flows, and so on, are determined at the business level, the integration of the business unit within the overall organization remains a critical element of business strategy.[141]

Horizontal and vertical integration are two forms of internal integration strategies selected by firms.[142] Harrigan argues that the horizontal or vertical configuring of the business is contingent on industry constraints including the phase of industry development, volatility of the competition, and bargaining power of the firm vis-à-vis suppliers, distributors, and customers.[143] While these factors are clearly important globally, other researchers, including Hymer, Dunning, Kindleberger, and Rugman, would argue that transaction cost efficiencies play a much more significant role in determining internal integration strategies.[144]

Internalization is frequently selected as the vehicle whereby firms strategically position themselves to capitalize on "international-type market imperfections."[145] Internalization involves removing a transaction from the marketplace and is largely based on a combination of several factors including supply security, improved coordination, economies of scale, monopolistic competition, and transaction cost efficiencies.[146] Perhaps the best definition of the internalization concept is provided by Teece:

> A transaction can be taken out of the market—that is, it can be internalized—and the specialized governance structure of the firm can be used to shield and protect the transaction and ensure full utilization of the specialized asset in question.[147]

In that internalization allows firms to transfer technology, capital resources, and organizational skills from one country to another, internalization implicitly involves both tangible asset transfers and intangible asset transfers.[148] Here Beamish and Banks assert that

> the economic reasoning supporting the internalization of markets in the case of vertical integration is concerned with the market in intermediate goods. In the case of horizontal diversification the concern is with the failure of markets in intangible assets for such things as management know-how, trade name or proprietary technology.[149]

If it were not for these market disequilibria (i.e., if international transaction markets were completely efficient), exporting would be the preferred strategy.[150] However, given the presence of market disequilibria, an internalization strategy can be designed to give the firm a competitive advantage in tangible and intangible asset transfers.

External Integration: The Importance of Coalitions. With the growth in international trade has come a paralleled growth in the use of coalitions as a means of implementing global strategies.[151] Coalitions can be defined as formal agreements linking one firm to another. While external integration strategies (both between firms and between businesses within the same corporate organization) are often approved at the corporate level, it is the business unit that typically instigates the relationship. No matter what the source, interbusiness coalitions are a clear element of global strategy.

Formal external integration strategies can take several forms including joint ventures, licensing agreements, supply agreements, and marketing/distribution agreements, among others.[152] While interbusiness integration strategies take several legal forms, the focus is on providing mutual benefits to the partners. These benefits, like those developed through internalization, also stem from competitive advantages achieved through tangible and intangible asset transfers.

The flow of tangible assets from one business to another principally involves two forms of coalitions: supply agreements and marketing/distribution agreements. Supply agreements link operations at the raw materials and intermediate products stage of production. Marketing/distribution agreements link organizations at the finished product stage of operations. Coalitions based on global distribution offer other economic advantages including circumventing national government investment and trade regulations, accessing national markets whose cultural idiosyncrasies would otherwise be intimidating, and reducing overall sales costs through the utilization of world-scale distribution networks.

Coalitions that exclusively exploit intangible asset transfers generally take the form of R&D partnerships and licensing agreements. Expenses for research and development can clearly be very high, and given the rapid acceleration in the diffusion of new technology, it is essentially impossible for any single business to maintain indefinitely a position of technological leadership in every related field. Thus, one type of intangible integration strategy involves the development of international information networks.[153]

Coalitions can provide not only access to new sources of technology but also new conduits for technology initially developed for a domestic or regional market. According to Ohmae:

> Since it costs dearly to develop a technologically advanced and differentiated product, the company must be able to sell simultaneously to the entire world in order to amortize the heavy front-end investment.[154]

Clearly, incentives can be strong for interfirm linkages at every stage of the value chain. The breadth of these linkages is dependent on the degree of correlation between tangible and intangible assets determined at the firm and industry levels. Variables associated with both internal and external integration strategies are found in Figure 2.4.

Investment Substrategies. Chandler was one of the first to articulate the importance that investment activities play in determining overall organi-

Figure 2.4
International Integration Substrategy Variables

VARIABLES	STUDIES
Keep international tangible asset flows (e.g. intermediate/finished products) in-house	Kindleberger (1969); Doz (1980); Crookell (1984); White and Poynter (1984); Harrigan (1985a); Porter (1980, 1985); Casson (1986); Flaherty (1986)
Keep international intangible asset flows (e.g. skills/technology) in-house	Kindleberger (1969); Hymer (1970); Johnson (1970); Rumelt (1974); Buckley and Casson (1976); Biggadike (1979); Doz (1980); Dunning (1981); Ohmae (1985); Porter (1985, 1986a) Flaherty (1986)
Vertically integrate operations	Hymer (1970); Williamson (1975); Buckley and Casson (1976); Calvet (1981); Harrigan (1985b); Beamish and Banks (1987)
Horizontally integrate operations	Hymer (1970); Williamson (1975); Buckley and Casson (1976); Calvet (1981); Perlmutter and Heenan (1986); Beamish and Banks (1987)
EXTERNAL INTEGRATION VARIABLES	
Secure longterm contractual agreements with buyers and sellers	Porter (1980, 1986a); Cvar (1984); Harrigan (1985, 1986); Ghemawat, Porter, and Rawlinson (1986); Perlmutter and Heenan
Establish formal international marketing/distribution agreements (e.g. joint ventures	Porter (1980); Ohmae (1985); Hamel and Prahalad (1985); Porter and Fuller (1986); Ghemawat, Porter, and Rawlinson (1986); Doz (1987)
Establish formal R & D sharing agreements (e.g. joint ventures/ licensing)	Porter (1980); Killing (1982); Cvar (1984); Harrigan (1985a); Ohmae (1985); Porter and Fuller (1986); Ghemawat, Porter, and Rawlinson (1986); Reich and Mankin (1986); Perlmutter and Heenan (1986); Doz (1987)
Establish formal international production sharing agreements	Ohmae (1985); Porter and Fuller (1986); Perlmutter and Heenan (1986); Reich and Mankin (1986)
Develop external international information networks	Buss (1982); Parsons (1983); Prahalad and Doz (1987); Lorange (1989)

tional strategy.[155] To Chandler, investment activities were equated with resource allocations. Ansoff expanded this work to include the organization's "growth vector" as a critical component of strategy.[156] Hofer and Schendel further refined this conceptualization of investment substrategies by (1) identifying resource deployments as a separate component of strategy and (2) suggesting the presence of autonomous organization investment substrategies.[157] According to Hofer and Schendel, a business unit's investment substrategy is typically "designed to support its competitive position strategy."[158] This is achieved through determining how resources are deployed within the business unit. In a global context, the business's investment substrategy is the chief vehicle for achieving virtually all the advantages of internal and external integration.

International investment substrategies are geared at concurrently achieving a competitive advantage while exploiting a host nation's comparative advantage.[159] Consequently, businesses competing in global industry contexts will, all things being equal, limit foreign direct investment (FDI) to those countries with (1) low cost factor endowments and (2) comparatively high national investment incentive levels. International competitors will also strive to minimize tax liabilities through favorable transfer pricing and the selection of remittance channels.

Internationally integrated business units have a unique capacity to access funds internationally that many strictly local firms do not have. Access to international funding is achieved through a combination of the business's association with its multinational corporation (MNC) parent and the business's involvement in and familiarity with multiple host nation capital and equity markets. Accessing funds internationally can be seen as a means to lower overall capital costs primarily through profiting from host nation financial market distortions. Variables associated with investment substrategies are shown in Figure 2.5.

Figure 2.5
International Investment Substrategy Variables

VARIABLES	STUDIES
Invest in countries with low cost resources (e.g., labor, raw materials)	Buckley and Casson (1976); Dunning (1980); Calvet (1981); Hout, Porter, and Rudden (1982); Cvar (1984); Kogut 1985b); Casson (1986); Porter (1986a, 1986b)
Invest in countries that offer investment incentives (e.g., low tariffs, grants)	Doz (1980, 1986); Porter (1980); Lindert and Kindleberger (1982); Cvar (1984); Lessard (1985); Encarnation and Wells (1986); Doz (1987)
Minimize tax liabilities through transfer pricing and choice of remittance channels	Rugman (1979); Lessard (1985); Srinivasan and Kim (1986); Prahalad and Doz (1987)
Source funds internationally	Rugman (1979); Doz (1980); Lessard (1985); Kogut (1985b); Porter (1986b)

SUMMARY

The purpose of this chapter has been to review the current literature governing the formulation of business strategies in global industries. To this end, strategy has been defined as the scope and competitive methods employed by an organization in order to "match" its skills, resources, and distinctive competencies with its competitive environment. The components of overall strategic behavior have been identified as including competitive position, political, and investment substrategies. The primary competitive environment of the business unit has been identified as the industry unit.

Seven empirical studies have been reviewed to determine how strategy has typically been operationalized in classification research as well as to identify which strategy variables are salient. In a domestic context, only competitive position substrategy variables were identified as discriminating.

The classification of patterns of strategic behavior in global industries has thus far received little attention in the literature. Indeed, while unique patterns of strategy are implicitly hypothesized to exist in global industries, little empirical support is available to indicate either the content or importance of these particular patterns. A further exploration of the methodology associated with uncovering the linkage of business strategy and the global industry contingency is the subject of Chapter 3.

NOTES

1. Drucker (1954).
2. Selznick (1957).
3. March and Simon (1958).
4. Chandler (1962).
5. Ansoff (1965).
6. This is exemplifed by Allan and Hammond (1975a, 1975b).
7. Hofer (1975: 786).
8. See Ansoff (1969) and Andrews (1971) for a broader discussion of the differences between strategic planning and strategy content from a more historical perspective.
9. While Bourgeois (1980b) presents an excellent overview of this issue, noted participants in the debate include Mintzberg (1973, 1987), Quinn (1981), Child (1972), Porter (1980), Harrigan (1980), Tregoe and Zimmerman (1980), Gupta and Govindarajan (1984), and Andrews (1987), among others.
10. Andrews (1987: 7).
11. See Hannan and Freeman (1977), Astley and Fombrun (1983), and Aldrich, McKelvey, and Ulrich (1984) for a more complete discussion of the population ecology perspective of the organization.

12. Astley and Fombrun (1983: 577).

13. Miles and Snow (1978), Mintzberg (1973, 1979a), Hambrick (1980), and Andrews (1987).

14. Schendel and Hofer (1979: 11).

15. Ibid.

16. See Allison (1969), Andrews (1971), Mintzberg (1979a), and J. Fry and Killing (1989) for frameworks that include goals in defining strategy.

17. Schendel and Hofer (1979).

18. See A. Morrison and Roth (1989).

19. Hofer and Schendel (1978: 25).

20. See Chrisman, Hofer, and Boulton (1988) for a more complete discussion of these two strategy components.

21. Schendel and Hofer (1979).

22. Hofer (1975), Hofer and Schendel (1978), Steiner (1979), Harrigan (1983), Ginsberg and Venkatraman (1985), Hambrick and Lei (1985), and Andrews (1987).

23. Ginsberg and Venkatraman (1985).

24. Hofer (1975).

25. See, for example, Emery and Trist (1965), Lawrence and Lorsch (1967), Thompson (1967), Osborn and Hunt (1974), and Downey, Hellriegel, and Slocum (1975).

26. Schendel and Hofer (1979).

27. Ginsberg and Venkatraman (1985).

28. Hofer (1975).

29. Singer (1961), Tilles (1966), Blau (1970), Andrews (1971), Williamson (1975), and D. Katz and Kahn (1978).

30. Lawrence and Lorsch (1967: 3–4).

31. Ansoff (1965: 80).

32. Tilles (1966).

33. R. Katz (1970).

34. Glueck (1972).

35. Child (1979: 394).

36. Scott (1973).

37. Ibid., p. 138.

38. Rumelt (1974: 12).

39. Pitts and Hopkins (1982).

40. Ibid., p. 23.

41. Rumelt (1974: 70).

42. Stopford and Wells (1972).

43. Daniels, Pitts, and Tretter (1984).

44. See ibid. and Stopford and Wells (1972).

45. Prahalad and Bettis (1986: 487).

46. Ibid., p. 494.

47. Tregoe and Zimmerman (1980).

48. Bartlett (1983).

49. Ibid., p. 140.

50. Bourgeois (1980b), Porter (1980), and Davis (1986).

51. Buzzell, Gale, and Sultan (1975) and Woo and Cool (1983).

52. Chrisman, Hofer, and Boulton (1988).
53. Hofer and Schendel (1978: 159).
54. Ibid.
55. Hambrick (1980), Snow and Hambrick (1980), Venkatraman and Grant (1986), and Herbert and Deresky (1987).
56. Hambrick (1980).
57. Miller and Friesen (1978) and Snow and Hambrick (1980).
58. Hambrick (1980).
59. Ibid., C. Galbraith and Schendel (1983), Harrigan (1983), and Porter (1985).
60. Buzzell, Gale, and Sulton (1975), Uterback and Abernathy (1975), Allan and Hammond (1975b), Hofer and Schendel (1978), Miles and Snow (1978), Henderson (1979), Wissema, Van der Pol, and Messer (1980), Porter (1980), Abell (1980), Doz (1980), Ohmae (1982), White and Poynter (1984), and Root (1987).
61. S. Hunt (1983), Hambrick (1984), and Chrisman, Hofer, and Boulton (1988).
62. McKelvey (1975), Porter (1985), Herbert and Deresky (1987), and Chrisman, Hofer, and Boulton (1988).
63. Wolf (1926).
64. S. Hunt (1983: 349).
65. Mayr (1982).
66. Chrisman, Hofer, and Boulton (1988: 415).
67. Harrigan (1983), Venkatraman and Grant (1986), Smith and Grimm (1987), and Miller (1987a).
68. Hofer and Schendel (1978). Also see Venkatraman and Grant (1986).
69. McKelvey (1975) and S. Hunt (1983).
70. McKelvey (1975: 509).
71. Hambrick (1984: 28).
72. Chrisman, Hofer, and Boulton (1988).
73. Hofer (1975).
74. See ibid., p. 798, and Levitt (1965).
75. Miller and Friesen (1978).
76. Porter (1980: 35).
77. Ibid., p. 41.
78. Dess and Davis (1984).
79. Woo and Cool (1983) and Roth (1986) raised concerns over the use of non-matched multiple respondents from a single firm.
80. White (1986).
81. Porter (1980).
82. Woo and Cool (1983).
83. Ibid., p. 17.
84. Robinson and Pearce (1988).
85. C. Galbraith and Schendel (1983).
86. Ibid., p. 158.
87. Chrisman, Hofer, and Boulton (1988).
88. Robinson and Pearce (1985).
89. Chrisman, Hofer, and Boulton (1987) are critical of this sample selection because small manufacturing firms are presumably all focused in scope, thus excluding a critical dimension of strategy from the study.

90. This previous work involved, among others, the work of Miles and Snow (1978), Hofer and Schendel (1978), Porter (1980), Bourgeois (1980a), Dess and Davis (1984), and Hambrick (1983c).

91. Davis (1986).

92. See Porter (1980) and Dess and Davis (1984).

93. Roth (1986).

94. Ibid., p. 64.

95. Ibid., p. 110.

96. Robinson and Pearce (1985).

97. Dess and Davis (1984).

98. Hofer and Schendel (1978).

99. Ibid.

100. Hambrick and Lei (1985: 765).

101. Hofer (1975), Hofer and Schendel (1978), Porter (1980), Harrigan (1980, 1983), Cvar (1984, 1986), and Andrews (1987).

102. Christensen et al. (1987: 231).

103. Prescott (1983: 129).

104. Porter (1980).

105. Ghoshal (1987).

106. Hout, Porter, and Rudden (1982) and Hamel and Prahalad (1985).

107. Dess (1987) and Keels et al. (1987).

108. Harrigan (1980, 1982), Yip (1982b), Hambrick and Scheter (1983), Zeithaml and Fry (1984), and Aaker and Day (1986).

109. Hout, Porter, and Rudden (1982), Hamel and Prahalad (1985), Cvar (1984), Porter (1986a), Bartlett (1986), Flaherty (1986), Doz (1987), and Jolly (1988).

110. For a more complete discussion of the globalization of buyer demand, see Levitt (1983) and Quelch and Hoff (1986).

111. See Davidson and Haspeslagh (1982), Hout, Porter, and Rudden (1982), Cvar (1984), Porter (1986a), Takeuchi and Porter (1986), and Prahalad and Doz (1987).

112. Hout, Porter, and Rudden (1982), Cvar (1984), Ohmae (1985), Hamel and Prahalad (1985), Porter (1986a), Chandler (1986), Bartlett (1986), Flaherty (1986), Doz (1987), Bartlett and Ghoshal (1987a), and Jolly (1988).

113. Prescott (1983), Cvar (1984), Ohmae (1985), Porter (1986a), Prahalad and Doz (1987), Doz (1987), Bartlett and Ghoshal (1987), and Jolly (1988).

114. Cvar (1984: 7).

115. Flaherty (1986).

116. See Doz (1980, 1987), Hout, Porter, and Rudden (1982), Prescott (1983), Cvar (1984), Hamel and Prahalad (1985), Chandler (1986), Ghoshal (1987), Porter (1986a), Takeuchi and Porter (1986), Yoshino (1986), Prahalad and Doz (1987), and Jolly (1988).

117. See Hout, Porter, and Rudden (1982) and Doz (1987).

118. Cvar (1984).

119. Porter (1980: 276).

120. Cvar (1984).

121. Prescott (1983) and Cvar (1984, 1986).

122. Ibid.

123. Porter (1986b: 29).

124. Prescott (1983).

125. Ibid.
126. Cvar (1986: 507).
127. Prescott (1983) and Cvar (1984, 1986).
128. Porter (1980).
129. Leontiades (1986).
130. Doz and Prahalad (1980) and Hamel and Prahalad (1985).
131. See Doz (1980), Bartlett (1985), Ghoshal (1987), and Prahalad and Doz (1987).
132. A. Morrison (1988).
133. Hofer and Schendel (1978). See also Chrisman, Hofer, and Boulton (1988).
134. A. Morrison and Roth (1989).
135. Ibid.
136. Chrisman, Hofer, and Boulton (1988).
137. Arndt (1983) and Boddewyn (1986).
138. Porter (1980) and Boddewyn (1986: 4).
139. See Ansoff (1965) for a discussion of the function that "rules" play in determining strategic behavior.
140. Kogut (1985a) and Porter (1985).
141. Harrigan (1986: 536).
142. Hymer (1970), Williamson (1975), Buckley and Casson (1976), Calvet (1981), Harrigan (1985b), Perlmutter and Heenan (1986), and Beamish and Banks (1987).
143. Harrigan (1985b: 404–406).
144. Hymer (1970), Dunning (1981), Kindleberger (1984), and Rugman (1985a, 1985b).
145. Rugman (1985a: 571).
146. Buckley and Casson (1976), Calvet (1981), Kindleberger (1984), Rugman (1985b), and Teece (1986).
147. Teece (1986: 24).
148. Kindleberger (1969), Johnson (1970), Hymer (1970), Buckley and Casson (1976), Dunning (1981), Casson (1986), and Porter (1986a, 1986b).
149. Beamish and Banks (1987: 2).
150. Rugman (1985a) and C. Galbraith and Kay (1986).
151. See Cvar (1984), Ohmae (1985), Ghemawat, Porter, and Rawlinson (1986), Porter and Fuller (1986), and Prahalad and Doz (1987) for a discussion of this phenomenon.
152. Porter and Fuller (1986).
153. Buss (1982), Parsons (1983), Lorange (1989), and Prahalad and Doz (1987).
154. Ohmae (1985: 17).
155. Chandler (1962).
156. Ansoff (1965).
157. Hofer and Schendel (1978).
158. Ibid., p. 159.
159. See Dunning (1981) and Porter (1986a).

CHAPTER 3

RESEARCH METHODOLOGY

The purpose of this chapter is to present the research methodology associated with the development of a classification of business strategies in global industries. Specifically, the chapter describes the methods employed to test for the relationship between conduct (competitive strategy) and performance within global industries, including both the strategy variable and sample selection process. Procedures discussed in the development of the classification include the use of principal components analysis, cluster analysis, and analysis of variance.

This chapter is divided into four main sections. The first section discusses the sample selection process including (1) the identification of global industries through a three-stage process, and (2) the selection of member businesses according to minimum-size criteria. The second section of the chapter examines the choice of the data collection instrument. In this section the advantages of using a combination of coarse-grained and fine-grained methodologies are discussed, given the particular research objectives. The third section of the chapter discusses the selection of strategy variables utilized in the classification procedure. Using the A. Morrison and Roth framework, 18 competitive positioning, 4 investment, 4 political, and 9 internal and external integration substrategy variables were identified.[1] Variable identification was modified through an extensive pretesting of the questionnaire instrument. The final section of the chapter describes the statistical methods used to classify both business strategy and performance in the identified global industries. The use of principal components analysis to reduce the original substrategy variables into a smaller set of strategy components is discussed. The use of principal component loadings as input to a cluster analysis algorithm as the basis of the strategy classification is also reviewed. Finally, constituent business performance ratings were then used to rank identified clusters.

SAMPLE SELECTION

A two-stage process was used in the sample selection. The first stage involved the identification of global industries. This was followed by identifying actual businesses competing in the selected global industries according to minimum-size criteria.

Identifying Global Industries

The specific global industries used in this study were identified through three separate steps. The use of multiple steps or measurements in strategy research has been recommended by Snow and Hambrick, Bourgeois, and Venkatraman and Grant.[2] As discussed in Chapter 2, the first step in the identification of global industries involved isolating an initial pool of global industries through a review of current literature on competition in global industries. When inconsistencies arose over levels of abstraction in identifying these industries, common references were made to the industries at four-digit SIC code levels. The identification of industries at the four-digit SIC level has been utilized by numerous researchers in operationalizing the competitive industry environment.[3]

In order to overcome the problem of varying degrees of "globalness" discussed in Chapter 2, the second step in the industry selection process involved identifying those industries with high levels of transnational trade flows. Only those industries where total imports and exports of product amounted to at least 50 percent of total U.S. consumption were considered. A combination of U.S. International Trade Commission and industry sources was used to isolate these industries. The summation of exports and imports as a percentage of consumption is used as an indication of the extent of integrated worldwide competition within the industry.[4] According to Porter, industries with high levels of cross-border trade flows in terms of imports and exports indicate a clear opportunity for the staggering of value activities across national borders to exploit comparative and competitive advantages.[5] Hence, summing import and export flows as a percentage of consumption is deemed the most appropriate way to capture the essence of this competitive environment. The 50 percent trade level is used to identify industries where at least half of the consumption is manifested by some form of international product flow. This level of transnational trade flow is consistent with levels identified by both Cvar and Ohmae and substantially surpasses levels identified by Prescott as characterizing autonomous industry classifications.[6] In all, 11 industries were identified from the larger pool of global industries.

The third stage in the industry identification process involved restricting this sample to industries that would minimize variance across the three key global industry parameters discussed in Chapter 2. These include: (1) intense levels of international competition, (2) competitors marketing a standardized product worldwide, and (3) the presence of competitors in all key international markets. An ANOVA procedure was used that compared within-group variance with variance separating different SIC code industries across the three different industry variables. These results are reported in Chapter 4.

Identifying Businesses Competing in Global Industries

The second stage in the sample selection process involved identifying businesses in each of the industries identified as global. The sample was designed to contain only divisional head offices (business units) and independent companies (businesses) within the identified global industries. Businesses and chief executives were identified through *America's Corporate Families* and *The Directory of Corporate Affiliations.* The sampling was limited to only those businesses with headquarters located within the United States.

Only those businesses with an excess of 150 employees and/or annual sales of at least $25 million were included in the sample. There are several reasons why these cutoff levels were used. Clear evidence is available in the literature that the strategic imperatives and resulting patterns of strategic behavior of small businesses differ significantly from those of medium and large businesses. For example, Miller and Toulouse argue that small size is "such a critical contingency for firms that it will create its own strategic and structural requirements."[7] Much of the rationale behind this dichotomy is that it is difficult for small businesses to achieve low costs through economies of scale or differentiate their products through marketing, both of which are factors essential to strategies in larger businesses.[8] Also, given that this study is intended to measure patterns of strategy varia-

Figure 3.1
Global Industries

INDUSTRY	SIC	TRADE RATIOS*	BUSINESSES IN ORIGINAL SAMPLE	NUMBER RESPONSES
Watches / Parts	3873	101.0%	9	1
Textile Machinery	3552	62.0%	17	9
Mining Machinery	3532	69.8%	36	16
Oilfield Machinery	3533	143.9%	43	19
Household Audio and Video Equipment	3651	95.7%	30	12
Semiconductors	3674	60.4%	63	26
Sewing Machines (Industrial & Household)	3636	106.3%	8	4
Electro-Medical & X-ray Apparatus	3693	58.6%	16	9
Synthetic Insecticides & Fungicides	2879	74.0%	22	16
Civil Aircraft	3721	121.9%	13	10
Civil Aircraft Parts (Including Engines)	3724/ 3728	69.4%	49	22
		TOTALS	306	144

* (Exports + Imports) / U.S. consumption

Source: U.S. International Trade Commission, "Summary of Trade and Tariff Information," USITC publications 841; and industry trade sources.

bles operationalized at the functional level, it was essential that the business units sampled be large enough to support viable functional departments. Thus, according to both Scott and Child, the sample would necessarily be limited to stage 2 firms—medium and large organizations.[9] Finally, recognizing that this study is intended to measure strategies of businesses that can potentially compete internationally and that the process of grading size levels is inherently subjective, a decision was made to limit sample size to those businesses associated with this minimum capacity.[10] Reviewing the sample identification sources indicated an apparent pattern in the onset of exporting at about the $25 million or 150 employee level.[11]

In all, 306 business units were identified in the initial sample. A listing of the industries/SIC codes identified, the number of businesses in each industry, and representative trade levels are found in Figure 3.1. As indicated in Figure 3.1, 144 businesses responded to the questionnaire. This represents a response rate of 47.1 percent. As suggested by Dillman, three separate mailings over a seven-week period were used to encourage a higher response rate.[12]

Figure 3.2
Key Business Unit Characteristics

AVERAGE TOTAL SALES	$912 MILLION
AVERAGE INTERNATIONAL SALES	$363 MILLION
AVERAGE NUMBER OF EMPLOYEES	5,387
AVERAGE NUMBER OF COUNTRIES WITH OPERATIONS	10

Of the original number of businesses responding, 13 were removed because both annual sales and number of employees were less than the identified limits for medium and large businesses, 11 were removed from the sample because annual sales were less than $25 million, and 5 were removed because the number of employees was less than 149. This resulted in a usable sample of 115 businesses. Several key business unit characteristics are summarized in Figure 3.2.

DATA COLLECTION INSTRUMENT

The objective of the data collection process is to provide the input necessary to develop a classification of business-level strategic behavior in global industries. Developing a cross-sectional classification of business strategies appropriately requires the selection of a research methodology that provides data that are highly generalizable and quantifiably differentiable.[13] Consistent with the classification methodologies employed by Robinson and Pearce, C. Galbraith and Schendel, Dess and

Davis, Davis, and Roth, a questionnaire was used as the principal form of data collection in this study.[14]

While this study relies heavily on input generated by questionnaire responses, it is recognized that multiple methodologies are preferred in determining the validity of classifications.[15] As a result, the business strategy taxonomy that is derived using questionnaire data was subjected to further confirmation and refinement through extensive follow-up interviews with a representative sample of classified businesses. The role of these follow-up interviews is more fully discussed in the fourth section of this chapter.

THE IDENTIFICATION OF STRATEGY VARIABLES

A multistage process was used in identifying relevant strategy variables associated with the competitive position, political, investment, and integration substrategies of the business units in the relevant sample. As discussed in Chapter 2, a major review was conducted of the strategy classification research. From this review, a group of 17 competitive position substrategy variables were identified and are presented in Figure 2.2. The identification of variables associated with the remaining political, investment, and integration substrategies of the sample businesses was also discussed in Chapter 2. A review of these variables is provided in Figure 3.3.

Pretesting the Instrument

With this group of variables representing four separate substrategy constructs, a review was conducted through field interviews to ascertain the comprehensiveness of the substrategy variables in capturing the essence of domestic and international business competition as well as to determine the objectivity of the wording of representative substrategy variables. The focus of the pretesting was the questionnaire generated from variables identified in Figures 2.2 and 3.3 The questionnaire also contained three measures of business unit performance.[16]

Two groups of individuals were involved in the pretest. The first contained academicians knowledgeable in the field of business strategy and familiar with the study's purpose and design. The purpose of this group was to scrutinize the questionnaire in terms of whether the study's objectives would be met and to suggest possible improvements in the overall design of the instrument.

Figure 3.3
International Substrategy Variables

<u>INVESTMENT SUBSTRATEGY VARIABLES</u>

1. Source capital funds internationally
2. Invest in countries with low costs
3. Invest in countries that offer investment incentives
4. Minimize tax liabilities through transfer pricing and method of cash remittance

<u>POLITICAL SUBSTRATEGY VARIABLES</u>

1. Use international political risk forecasting
2. Utilize political skills to lobby for favorable foreign government policies
3. Safeguard operations from foreign intervention
4. Secure assistance of U.S. government / agencies in penetrating foreign markets

<u>INTEGRATION SUBSTRATEGY VARIABLES</u>
(Internal)

1. Internationally control the manufacturing cycle from raw materials to distribution of finished product
2. Control within the organization the international transfer of intangible assets
3. Vertically integrate operations worldwide
4. Horizontally integrate operations worldwide

(External)

1. Secure longterm contractual agreements with international buyers / sellers
2. Utilize formal international marketing agreements with outside firms
3. Utilize formal international R & D sharing/technology sharing agreements with outside firms
4. Utilize formal international production sharing agreements with outside firms

5. Develop external international information networks

The second pretest group consisted of people drawn from

The second pretest group consisted of people drawn from the identified sample being surveyed. In all, seven executives representing five businesses in four of the identified industries (civil aircraft parts, synthetic insecticides and fungicides, mining machinery, and textile machinery) were interviewed. Average time spent in each interview was approximately one and a half hours. During the interviews, executives were asked open-ended questions regarding the clarity and objectivity of each questionnaire item, the overall comprehensiveness of the instrument in capturing the variance of each respondent's business strategy, and appropriate measures and ranges of business unit performance. Respondents were also questioned for suggestions on improving the overall design of the instrument.

As a result of the instrument pretesting, significant improvements were made in the wording of several questionnaire items. While the comprehensiveness of the four constructs designed to measure business unit strategy was generally affirmed, important changes and revisions were also suggested within both the political and external integration substrategy dimensions. These changes have been reflected in Figure 3.3. In addition, there was general agreement on the need to add one more variable—the importance of utilizing a highly skilled sales force/agents—to capture competitive positioning more effectively. Given that this variable was not considered as discriminating in the previously cited taxonomic research, it is not found in Figure 2.2. It was, however, included on the questionnaire. A sample of the complete questionnaire is found in Appendix A.

THE CLASSIFICATION PROCESS

With the identification of a group of 115 businesses competing in global industries, questionnaire responses were subjected to a variety of both qualitative and quantitative procedures in developing the classification. These procedures included five broad steps that are shown in Figure 3.4 and discussed below.

The first step focused on refining the substrategy constructs through the development of strategic factors. In the development of strategic factors, principal components analysis was used independently on variables associated with each of the four substrategy constructs. Factors were interpreted by rotating the factor matrix and assessing variable loadings.

With the identification of separate factors, the second step in the classification process involved the identification of actual patterns of business-level strategic behavior, or patterns of strategic factors. This was carried out through the clustering of the identified businesses based on their respective factor scores. Both hierarchical and nonhierarchical clustering algorithms were used in this procedure.

The third step in the classification process involved labeling the clusters. Here it was appreciated that several measures would be of assistance. Initially, clusters were identified by analyzing factor score means for each cluster. To assist in the labeling, an analysis of variance procedure was used on the cluster means of each of the high-loading strategy variables. This procedure allowed for the clarification of each cluster's identity based

Figure 3.4
Steps in the Classification Process

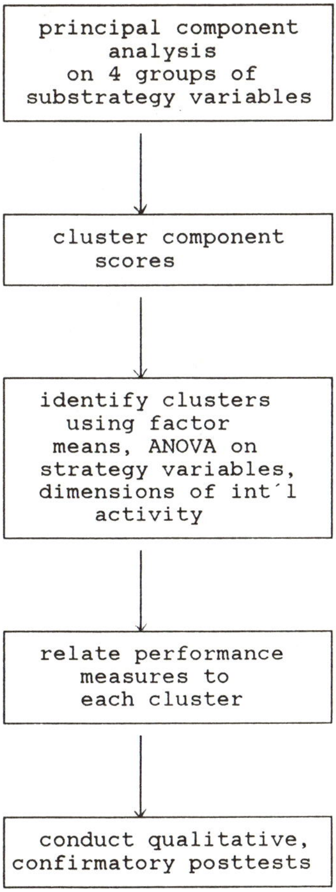

on comparisons between emphasis placed on individual strategy variables. As a final tool in labeling the clusters, several measures of international activity were used. These measures included a determination of the mean number of countries with subsidiaries or joint ventures, total business sales, total international sales, total international sales as a percentage of total business sales, foreign operating profit as a percentage of total profits, and foreign assets as a percentage of total assets for each cluster. The determination of these measures was based on questionnaire responses.

The fourth step in the classification process involved the assessment of relative performance levels for each identified pattern of strategic behavior. Performance measures included average three-year return on assets, average three-year return on investment, and average three-year annual sales growth. These performance measures were all commonly utilized in the strategy classification research reviewed in Chapter 2 and were confirmed in the pretest as being critical performance criteria to each business unit.

While multivariate classification procedures are extremely useful in the development of strategy classification, it would be difficult and premature to draw definitive conclusions exclusively from their use. Indeed, it has been suggested that multivariate classification procedures should be accompanied by more qualitative measures of business strategy in order to substantiate construct validity.[17] The importance of combining multiple sources of measurement in strategy research has been strongly advocated in the literature.[18] Combining multiple strategy measures not only can serve as confirmation of the empirically derived taxonomy but also can assist in providing more detailed and specific descriptions of the clusters.

As a result of the need to combine methodological tools, following the empirical classification of business strategies, confirmatory posttests were conducted to assist in both validating and clarifying the classification. The posttest first involved appealing to secondary data on the strategic conduct of different businesses representing each of the four clusters. This was followed by interviews with executives from a representative group of businesses identified in each strategy cluster.

The importance of using posttests in the classification procedure is particularly pronounced in bridging the gap between the identification of strategic factors and the clarification of the cluster solution. As such, posttests were conducted to confirm and clarify the classification; they were not designed to derive independently a classification through the codification and analysis of data.

SUMMARY

In the development of a classification of business strategies in global industries, 11 industries have tentatively been identified as global. From these industries, an initial sample of 115 medium and large businesses has been identified for the sample. Further tests to determine the homogeneity of both the industry groups and sample businesses are reported in Chapter 4.

Chapter 4 also provides the foundation for the development of an empirical classification of business strategies in global industries. A combination of principal components analysis, cluster analysis, and analysis of variance was used in combination with secondary and posttest interview data in the development of the classification. Chapter 5 serves as a foundation for a more in-depth investigation of the classification.

NOTES

1. See A. Morrison and Roth (1988) for a more complete discussion of the four-dimensional framework.
2. Snow and Hambrick (1980), Bourgeois (1984), and Venkatraman and Grant (1986).
3. Porter (1980), C. Galbraith and Schendel (1983), Prescott (1983), Hambrick (1983b), Dess and Davis (1984), Gomes-Casseras (1985), and Dess (1987).
4. Cvar (1984).
5. Porter (1986b).
6. Cvar (1984), Ohmae (1985), and Prescott (1983).
7. Miller and Toulouse (1986: 47).
8. Buzzell, Gale, and Sultan (1975), Henderson (1979), Porter (1980), and Miller and Toulouse (1986).
9. Scott (1973) and Child (1979).
10. McKinsey & Company (1987).
11. In some instances data were available for only one of these measurements.
12. Dillman (1978).
13. See Hambrick (1980), Harrigan (1983), and Bonoma (1985).
14. See Robinson and Pearce (1985), C. Galbraith and Schendel (1983), Dess and Davis (1984), Davis (1986), and Roth (1986).
15. Jick (1979), Snow and Hambrick (1980), Bourgeois (1984), and Venkatraman and Grant (1986).
16. Performance indicators selected included after-tax return on total assets, after-tax return on total investment, and annual increase in total sales. These performance measures were most commonly utilized in the classification research cited in Chapter 2.
17. Hambrick (1984), Bourgeois (1984), and Venkatraman and Grant (1986).
18. Hambrick (1980), Snow and Hambrick (1980), Montgomery (1982), Harrigan (1983), and Venkatraman and Grant (1986).

CHAPTER 4

DATA ANALYSIS AND STATISTICAL RESULTS

The purpose of this chapter is to develop a taxonomy of business strategies in global industries and to determine the relative success of these strategies in a global industry context. As described in Chapter 3, the analytical procedures include: (1) the selection of a group of global industries and constituent businesses; (2) the refinement of the four substrategy constructs through principal components analysis to create a set of representative strategic factors; (3) the identification of patterns of strategic behavior through cluster analysis based on the identified strategic factors; and (4) the assessment of relative performance levels for each identified pattern of strategic behavior.

The chapter is organized in sections that are devoted to each of these analytical procedures. Beyond empirically identifying patterns of strategic behavior, Chapter 4 also provides the qualitative review of business strategies in global industries through the posttesting of the derived classification. This provides the foundation for a more thorough international business strategy theory building section, which is the subject of Chapter 5.

THE SELECTION OF GLOBAL INDUSTRIES AND CONSTITUENT BUSINESSES

In Chapter 3, 11 industries were identified as global through both a review of the literature and an inspection of international trade flow levels.

As a final stage in the identification of global industries, SIC code industry means were compared across three key global industry parameters. As discussed in Chapter 2, these variables included (1) intensity of international competition, (2) the presence of competitors marketing a standardized product worldwide, and (3) the presence of competitors that have a presence in all key international markets. Means were examined using an ANOVA procedure that compared within-group variance with variance separating the 11 different SIC code industries. These results are reported in Appendix B. In each instance, no significant differences ($p > 0.05$) were found in SIC code industry emphasis across each of the three global industry parameters. Therefore, all 11 SIC code industries identified in Chapter 3 were deemed global industries for the study.

Pooling SIC Code Industry Responses

With the identification of 11 global industries, an ANOVA procedure was performed to assess whether particular SIC code industries placed unique emphasis on each of the 35 strategy variables shown in Figures 2.2 and 3.2. The results of this procedure are shown in Appendix C. The appropriateness of pooling individual global industry responses would be called into question if it was found that emphasis on strategy variables was idiosyncratic to particular industries. Here, no significance ($p > 0.05$) was found between SIC code industry means with 32 of the 35 variables. However, differences were evident between SIC code industry emphasis on (1) the importance of investing in countries with low costs, (2) the importance of utilizing political skills to lobby for favorable foreign government policies, and (3) the importance of minimizing taxes through transfer pricing.

In the three cases where significant differences were evident, further paired comparisons of SIC group means were performed using the Scheffe multiple comparison method as suggested by Pfaffenberger and Patterson.[1] Comparison tests are useful for exploring which pairs of industries place significantly different emphasis on a given strategy variable. The Scheffe multiple comparison method has been viewed as being superior to simple t-tests to the degree that confidence intervals for each contrast are based on F-values for the entire sample.[2] Here, no paired comparisons were significantly different at the 0.05 level across the SIC code industries for any of the three variables. This suggests that differences between SIC code industry emphasis resulted from incorrect simultaneous confidence intervals across groups of SIC code industries rather than actual paired individual industries. Given these results, it appeared appropriate to pool the responses across the 11 SIC code industries.

THE REFINEMENT OF SUBSTRATEGY CONSTRUCTS

Consistent with the conceptualization of international business strategy discussed in Chapter 2, principal components analysis was performed independently on variables associated with the competitive positioning, international investment, international political, and international integration substrategy constructs. This resulted in a pattern of loadings that were used to identify each strategic factor. Principal components analysis was used after an initial inspection of the correlation matrix revealed that significant intercorrelations existed among the variables. This suggested that a smaller number of factors may underlie the larger set of variables associated with each substrategy construct.

The objective of principal components analysis is to transform an "original set of variables into a smaller set of linear combinations that account for most of the variance of the original set."[3] As a data reduction technique, principal components analysis has been used by a variety of strategy researchers including C. Galbraith and Schendel, White, Douglas and Rhee, and Miller.[4] In exploratory strategic management research, principal components analysis may also be more appropriate in that strategy is regarded as being a function of its indicators (i.e., strategy variables), rather than the variables being regarded as a function of the strategy, which is the case with factor analysis.

Principal components analysis considers the total variance contained in a set of variables. The total variance is extracted from the correlation matrix provided through a standardization of the original set of variables. Standardization assures that the variance associated with no one variable dominates component loadings. From the correlation matrix, principal components are extracted where eigenvalues represent the amount of total variance accounted for by each component. As such, "each observation is made up of a linear combination of the principal components."[5] The eigenvalue for each principal component represents the variance of each component. Variance is maximized by the first principal component such that no linear combination of the original variables will explain more variance than the first principal component.[6]

Principal components are most appropriately interpreted by computing the component loadings that represent the correlations between variables and respective principal components. The rotation of factors has commonly been advocated to assist in interpreting the patterning of variables. According to Hair, Anderson, and Tatham:

> The ultimate effect of rotating the factor matrix is to redistribute the variance from earlier factors to later ones to achieve a simpler, theoretically more meaningful, factor pattern.[7]

Of the various rotation methods, VARIMAX has been commonly suggested as the most appropriate orthogonal rotation for simplifying columns of the factor matrix.[8]

As suggested by Kim and Mueller, and Dillon and Goldstein, components were independently derived for each of the four substrategy constructs.[9] Although with both the international political and international investment substrategies little benefit could be anticipated in terms of data reduction, it was recognized that the application of the principal components analysis procedure would provide (1) verification that a single strategy construct was representative of each of the associated strategy variables and (2) consistent input in a cluster analysis algorithm performed in a metric space with orthogonal dimensions.[10] Furthermore, by clustering factor scores, each component, whether representative of unidimensional or multidimensional substrategy constructs, receives equal weight in the cluster procedure.[11] This is most appropriate, particularly at an exploratory level, given the inability to determine appropriate factor weightings independently. The rationale for using cluster analysis to group businesses according to common emphasis placed on identified factors is more fully discussed later in the chapter.

Although no exact quantitative method exists for determining the appropriate number of components to be extracted, two procedures have been commonly used. Several researchers have suggested the extraction of principal components with eigenvalues greater than one.[12] The rationale for the eigenvalue criterion, according to Hair, Anderson, and Tatham, "is that any individual factor should account for at least the variance of a single variable if it is to be retained for interpretation."[13] Researchers have also advocated the use of scree tail tests in conjunction with minimum eigenvalue tests.[14] These tests provide visual evidence of systemic changes in principal component variance with the number of components retained.

Competitive Positioning Factors

Based on both the minimum eigenvalue criterion and scree tail tests, the principal components analysis resulted in the identification of 5 factors from the original 18 competitive positioning variables shown in Figure 2.2. These five factors accounted for 64.0 percent of total variance. Rotated component loadings are found in Figure 4.1. All 18 competitive positioning variables exhibited factor loadings of greater than or equal to +/– 0.45. Factor loadings of +/– 0.45 are consistent with cutoff levels used by Miller and Friesen, Dess and Davis, Robinson and Pearce, and Davis and exceed the minimum 0.30 levels suggested by D. Morrison.[15] The +/– 0.45 cutoff criterion also adheres to levels Kim and Mueller regard as "conservative."[16]

The factor loadings for each of the identified principal components represent five internally consistent strategic factors. *Factor 1* appears to be

Figure 4.1
Rotated Component Loadings for Competitive Position Strategy Variables

	FACTORS				
VARIABLES	F 1	F 2	F 3	F 4	F 5
New product development	0.246	0.082	0.363	0.586	-0.151
Control overhead	0.140	0.258	0.234	-0.410	-0.491
Brand identification	0.552	-0.039	0.494	0.204	-0.111
Customer service	0.678	0.025	0.267	0.127	-0.068
Innovative manufacturing	0.039	0.808	0.092	0.171	-0.268
Control dist. channels	-0.205	0.118	0.730	0.098	0.007
Product quality	0.859	0.098	-0.040	0.003	0.078
Marketing innovation	0.335	0.053	0.732	0.161	0.024
Low pricing	0.085	0.299	0.251	-0.612	-0.225
Monitor market	0.516	0.436	0.463	-0.092	-0.099
Capacity utilization	-0.021	0.727	0.154	-0.096	0.148
Specialty products	0.081	0.199	0.221	0.595	0.114
Skilled labor	0.544	0.329	0.032	-0.203	0.197
Industry reputation	0.820	0.126	0.090	0.090	-0.112
High-priced products	0.030	0.056	0.139	0.078	0.877
Modern plant & equip.	0.209	0.781	-0.006	0.124	0.196
Manufacturing efficiency	0.201	0.794	0.025	-0.132	-0.175
Skilled sales force	0.389	0.079	0.709	-0.142	0.134
EIGENVALUE	3.224	2.978	2.463	1.489	1.362

DESCRIPTIVE TITLE OF STRATEGY COMPONENTS

FACTOR 1: Quality Reputation

FACTOR 2: Manufacturing Prowess

FACTOR 3: Marketing Prowess

FACTOR 4: Product Specialization

FACTOR 5: Prestige Products

a *quality reputation* aspect of competitive positioning. This is suggested by the two variables with the highest factor loadings, 0.859 for "product quality" and 0.820 for "industry reputation." Further support is provided by very high loadings on "utilizing skilled labor" (0.544), "emphasizing customer service" (0.678), and "building brand identification" (0.552). These are all variables associated with a competitive positioning strategy based on maintaining a positive industry reputation. However, there was one variable, "monitoring market opportunities" (0.516), that, although loading highly on Factor 1, seemed inconsistent with maintaining or developing quality reputation. This same variable also loaded highly on Factor 3, which is more closely associated with the marketing activities of businesses.

Factor 2 shows high factor loadings on the four variables associated with *manufacturing prowess*. These include an emphasis on "promoting innovative manufacturing" (0.808), "promoting manufacturing efficiency" (0.794), "emphasizing modern plant and equipment" (0.781), and "emphasizing high-capacity utilization" (0.727). This second factor appears to be associated with competitive positioning based on manufacturing skills and resources.

Factor 3 shows a clear emphasis on *marketing prowess*. Three variables, "controlling distribution channels" (0.730), "developing innovative marketing techniques" (0.732), and "utilizing highly skilled sales force" (0.709), all are highly correlated with this factor. Two other variables, "building brand identification" (0.494) and "monitoring market opportunities" (0.463), while also loading on Factor 1, load significantly on Factor 3 and contribute in its interpretation as a marketing process dimension of competitive positioning.

Factor 4 is indicative of a *product specialization* component of competitive positioning. Innovative products are negatively correlated with "low pricing" (–0.612) and highly correlated with both "new product development" (0.586) and "emphasizing specialty products" (0.595). This strategic factor appears strongly associated with competitive positioning based on the nature of specialized products offered.

Factor 5, *prestige products*, is positively correlated with "producing high-priced products for market niches" (0.877) and negatively correlated with "tightly controlling costs" (–0.491). High margins on high-priced products decrease pressures for being the low-cost producer. Competitive positioning based on prestige products is representative of a high-price market niche strategy.

International Investment Factor

Only one factor was derived from the four international investment variables. Loadings associated with this factor are found in Figure 4.2 The use of rotation to assist in factor interpretation is not possible with only one factor. However, all four variables do load significantly on the construct, indicating high intercorrelations among the variables. Principal components analysis can assist in identifying the relative importance of each variable to the construct. In this case, the presence of investment incentives in potential host countries and the ability to minimize taxes through transfer pricing appeared to dominate international investment strategy.

Figure 4.2
Component Loadings for International Investment Strategy Variables

VARIABLE	FACTOR
Source funds internationally	0.619
Invest in low-cost countries	0.610
Invest in countries with investment incentives	0.862
Minimize taxes through transfer pricing	0.843
EIGENVALUE	2.208

International Political Factors

Like the variables loading on the international investment factor, only one international political factor was identified. These loadings are found in Figure 4.3. Three of the four component variables loaded highly on this factor: "lobbying for favorable foreign government policies" (0.813), "using international political risk forecasting" (0.747), and "securing the assistance of the U.S. government in penetrating foreign markets" (0.696). "Safeguarding operations from foreign intervention" was not shown to be highly correlated with the international political strategy construct of the sample businesses.

International Integration Factors

External and internal integration, although discussed separately, are both components of the international integration construct. Consequently, the

Figure 4.3
Component Loadings for International Political Strategy Variables

VARIABLE	FACTOR
Political risk forecasting	0.747
Lobby foreign governments	0.813
Secure U.S. government assistance	0.696
Avoid foreign intervention	0.449
EIGENVALUE	1.903

Figure 4.4
Rotated Component Loadings for International Integration Strategy Variables

VARIABLE	FACTOR 1	FACTOR 2
Internationally control manufacturing	0.810	0.027
Control int'l transfer of intangible assets	0.719	0.102
Vertically integrate operations worldwide	0.758	0.045
Horizontally integrate operations worldwide	0.544	0.246
Long-term agreements with buyers/sellers	0.498	0.382
Utilize external marketing agreements	0.019	0.846
Utilize external R&D agreements	0.274	0.700
Utilize external production agreements	0.022	0.811
Develop external information networks	0.279	0.453
EIGENVALUE	2.446	2.289
DESCRIPTIVE TITLE OF STRATEGY COMPONENT	Int'l Internal Integration	Int'l External Integration

nine internal and external integration variables were pooled in the development of principal components. The principal components analysis resulted in the identification of two factors. The rotated component loadings are found in Figure 4.4.

Consistent with the conceptualization of the international integration construct, the factor loadings indicate a strong agreement with the preliminary partition of the construct into internal and external dimensions. *Factor 1* is clearly associated with *international internal integration* of business activities. Four of the five variables that load highly on Factor 1 are all directly associated with different dimensions of internalization: "internationally control the manufacturing cycle from raw materials to distribution of finished product" (0.810), "internationally control the international transfer of intangible assets" (0.719), "vertically integrate operations worldwide" (0.758), and "horizontally integrate operations worldwide" (0.544). However, the fifth variable, "securing long-term agreements with international buyers/sellers" (0.498), was not as strongly stressed. Perhaps long-term agreements with buyers and/or sellers are necessary to mitigate some of the risk associated with the worldwide integration of operations.

Factor 2 shows high factor loadings on the four variables associated with *external international integration.* "Utilizing external international marketing agreements" (0.846), "utilizing external international R&D sharing agreements" (0.700), "utilizing external international production-sharing agreements" (0.811), and "developing external international information networks" (0.453) all load highly on this factor.

IDENTIFICATION OF COMPOSITE BUSINESS STRATEGIES IN GLOBAL INDUSTRIES

Conceptually, the classification of business strategies is based on identifying discrete groups of businesses emphasizing similar patterns of strategic behavior. These patterns are associated with common emphasis groups of businesses place on each of the nine identified strategic factors. Consequently, in order to develop an empirical classification of business strategies in global industries, a method of grouping the nine identified strategic factors was required. Cluster analysis was selected because of its frequent use as a statistical method of classification. Indeed, according to Punj and Stewart, "Cluster analysis provides one, empirically based, means for explicitly classifying objects. Such a tool is particularly relevant for . . . emerging discipline[s]."[17]

The objective of cluster analysis is to group objects into groups according to their closeness in n-dimensional space.[18] The success of the classification procedure is contingent on objects within a group being more similar—having less variance—than objects in other groups.[19]

Cluster analysis has served as a useful tool in assisting strategic management researchers in partitioning groups of competitors based on each group pursuing a similar patttern of strategic behavior. Gale, who was one of the first strategy researchers to use this procedure, clustered competitors in terms of financial and business risk.[20] Others using cluster analysis to group competitors include Hatten, C. Galbraith and Schendel, Hambrick, Dess and Davis, Harrigan, Davis, Smith and Grimm, and Robinson and Pearce.[21] Both Hambrick and Prescott have also used cluster analysis to partition competitive environments.[22]

The basis of cluster analysis is the partitioning of objects according to some measure of similarity. Most commonly this involves the partitioning of n-dimensional space according to the Euclidian distance between objects.[23] Clustering, in this case, is based on composite factor scores for each observation. Factor scores represent "the degree to which each individual scores high on the group of items that load high on a factor."[24] The clustering represents an attempt to group observations according to common building blocks represented by the computed factor scores.

Several clustering algorithms can be used in the classification process. Common among these algorithms is the attempt to minimize within-group variance and maximize between-group variance. Beyond this common base, two broad groups of clustering algorithms are most frequently used: hierarchical and nonhierarchical. Hierarchical clustering procedures proceed with no preselected number of clusters or seeds. Agglomerative hierarchical procedures begin by considering each object as a separate cluster and proceed by fusing clusters based on proximity criteria. This grouping procedure continues until all objects are contained within a single cluster. However, unlike nonhierarchical clustering, the assignment of an object to a cluster is irrevocable.[25]

Nonhierarchical cluster procedures, often referred to as iterative partitioning methods, have the advantage of permitting the reallocation of cluster assignments through the sequential partitioning of the data. The result is a group of algorithms that appear

> to be more robust than any of the hierarchical methods with respect to the presence of outliers, error perturbations of the distance measures and the choice of a distance metric. . . . . [Indeed,] empirical

> studies of the performance of clustering algorithms suggest that one of the iterative partitioning methods is preferable to the hierarchical methods.[26]

Unfortunately, "the use of partitioning techniques usually assumes that the number of final clusters is known and specified in advance."[27] In addition, nonhierarchical clustering results are improved when nonrandom initial cluster seeds are specified.

Recognizing the advantages and disadvantages of both the hierarchical and nonhierarchical approaches, several authors have suggested a two-stage approach to clustering, which was used in this study.[28] The first stage involved the development of a preliminary cluster solution using one of the hierarchical procedures. This facilitated the identification and elimination of outliers and assisted in the selection of the appropriate number of clusters and cluster seeds. This information was then used as the basis of nonhierarchical analysis for cluster refinement.

Preliminary Cluster Solution

The centroid method of hierarchical clustering was used in the development of a preliminary cluster solution. Unlike other hierarchical methods, centroid clustering is best suited for metric data, an outcome of the principal components procedure previously discussed. Centroid clustering bases groupings according to the Euclidian distance between cluster means (centroids), which migrate as clusters merge.

Outliers. Using the centroid method, three outliers were identified. These included observations from the synthetic insecticide and fungicide industry (SIC code 2879), the mining machinery industry (SIC code 3532), and the oilfield machinery industry (SIC code 3533). The presence of these outliers was confirmed using the nonhierarchical SAS FASTCLUS procedure and specifying an artificially high number of clusters to detect single-member clusters. These three observations were then eliminated from the sample.[29]

Number of Clusters. The centroid clustering method was also used as a basis for identifying the number of clusters to be selected. At the outset it should be clear that no purely objective procedure currently exists for determining cluster boundaries or the appropriate number of clusters.[30] Rather, a combination of formal tests and subjective measures is most frequently used.

Ultimately, the selection of an appropriate number of clusters can be viewed as a trade-off between parsimony and detail.[31] Increasing the number of clusters results in tighter clusters (less within-group variance), but as a data reduction and classification tool its purpose is defeated if each observation ends up as a cluster. Judgment is required in weighing this trade-off. To assist in this process, several general guidelines have been suggested. Lehmann asserts that reliable clusters from survey data fall in an n/30 to n/50 range.[32] This would call for a 3- or 4-cluster solution. Others have suggested looking for pronounced changes in cluster tightness as evidenced by changes in normalized centroid distance, R^2 (between cluster sum of squares divided by total sample sum of squares), and pseudo-F as the algorithm shifts from one clustering solution to another.[33]

Using these criteria, a four-cluster solution was judged most meaningful. Two-, three-, and five-cluster solutions were also investigated using both hierarchical and nonhierarchical procedures. The nonhierarchical procedure used in the final clustering was SAS FASTCLUS. The advantage of using this procedure is the algorithm's ability to replace initial seeds—thus reducing the importance of initial seed selection—based on different tests of observation distances to existing seeds and distances separating existing seeds.

As the number of clusters increased from two to five, different strategic patterns became evident. At the two- and three-cluster solutions, patterns of strategic behavior were so broad as to be difficult to interpret meaningfully. The two-cluster solution was particularly problematic with little conceptual interpretability. The three-cluster solution resulted in one cluster strongly representative of a domestic quality reputation strategy. However, the two remaining clusters were difficult to differentiate. Both strongly emphasized global integration, manufacturing prowess, and marketing prowess. While parsimonious, the three-cluster lacked a certain richness in interpretability. In contrast, the five-cluster solution resulted in the partitioning of one of the clusters from the four-cluster solution into a fifth, unfocused strategy cluster. However, beyond this, the four remaining clusters stayed consistent with the four-cluster solution. There was also concern over the reliability of a five-cluster solution, given Lehmann's criterion.[34] In addition to the problems of interpretability, each of the two-, three-, and five-cluster solutions resulted in inferior clusters in terms of pseudo-F and overall cluster tightness.

To assess further the validity of the four-cluster solution, a comparison was made of the SIC code industry composition of each cluster. This is an important comparison in that the clusters could simply be composed of single SIC code industries or groups of similar SIC code industries as opposed to separate groups of businesses emphasizing discrete patterns of strategic behavior in global industries. Using a chi-square test, the proportion of respondents from each SIC code industry was not found to vary significantly ($p > 0.05$) among the four clusters. These results are reported in Appendix D.

Descriptions of the Four Clusters

The four clusters represent discrete patterns of business-level strategic behavior in global industries. By examining the cluster means for each of the nine strategic factors, descriptive labels were identified for the four clusters. Factor means are presented in Figure 4.5. To assist further in interpreting the distinguishing attributes of each cluster, an analysis of variance procedure was conducted on the cluster means of each of the high-loading strategy variables. These strategy variable means are found in Figure 4.6. The F-values shown in Figure 4.6 should not be considered a statistical test of the differences between clusters.[35] However, the test does indicate where significant differences occur between clusters and can, as a consequence, provide useful assistance in cluster interpretation. In addition, comparisons of mean levels of international activity among the clusters are found in Figure 4.7. A more complete discussion of cluster differences is found in Chapter 5.

Figure 4.5
Cluster Means of Strategic Factors

	CLUSTER1	CLUSTER2	CLUSTER3	CLUSTER4
QUALITY REPUTATION	5.549	6.209	5.319	5.814
MANUFACTURING PROWESS	6.207	3.808	5.077	6.392
MARKETING PROWESS	5.042	4.641	5.486	6.002
PRODUCT SPECIALIZATION	1.299	-0.057	0.940	0.535
PRESTIGE PRODUCTS	0.752	-0.415	1.972	1.493
INT´L INVESTMENT	1.948	3.484	4.111	6.121
INT´L POLITICAL	2.928	5.304	3.726	6.439
INT´L INTERNAL INTEGR.	2.918	3.297	4.024	5.763
INT´L EXTERNAL INTEGR.	2.074	4.393	4.390	5.133
	(n=11) (9.8%)	(n=19) (17.0%)	(n=43) (38.4%)	(n=39) (34.8%)

Figure 4.6
Four-Cluster Solution: Strategy Means

STRATEGY VARIABLE	CLUSTER1	CLUSTER2	CLUSTER3	CLUSTER4	F-VALUE[a]
QUALITY REPUTATION					
Brand identification	5.363	4.684	4.698	5.590	2.71**
Customer service	5.909	6.263	6.023	6.205	0.42
Product quality	6.364	6.474	6.326	6.538	0.45
Monitor market	5.454	4.737	5.163	5.846	3.95**
Skilled labor	4.000	4.158	4.326	5.308	4.56**
Industry reputation	6.182	6.316	5.535	6.385	5.77***
MANUFACTURING PROWESS					
Innovative manufacturing	5.818	4.105	4.302	5.615	10.73***
Capacity utilization	4.909	2.632	4.238	5.462	17.93***
Modern plant & equip.	5.545	3.000	4.442	5.421	15.11***
Manufacturing efficiency	6.000	5.105	5.209	6.154	6.41***
MARKETING PROWESS					
Control dist. channels	3.636	2.895	4.023	4.846	5.94***
Marketing innovation	4.909	4.474	4.930	5.513	2.68**
Skilled sales force	5.273	5.211	5.558	5.846	1.22
PRODUCT SPECIALIZATION					
New product development	5.909	5.316	5.558	5.821	0.70
Low pricing	4.727	4.500	3.744	4.921	3.97**
Specialty products	5.091	3.526	5.024	4.872	4.31**
PRESTIGE PRODUCTS					
Tightly control costs	5.273	6.158	5.442	5.949	2.63*
High-priced products	4.455	3.368	5.619	5.051	12.06***
INTERNATIONAL INVESTMENT					
Source funds int'lly	1.778	2.684	2.930	4.351	9.64***
Low-cost countries	1.800	2.474	3.209	4.308	7.94***
Country incentives	1.100	2.263	2.814	4.378	20.75***
Transfer pricing	2.100	3.053	3.419	5.211	16.04***
INTERNATIONAL POLITICAL					
Risk forecasting	1.800	2.737	2.349	4.162	19.56***
Lobby governments	1.600	4.368	2.558	4.631	20.52***
Government assistance	1.500	4.263	2.419	4.211	15.20***
INT'L INTERNAL INTEGRATION					
Control manufacturing	2.500	2.474	2.605	4.667	14.39***
Intangible assets	2.900	3.368	3.744	5.184	9.12***
Vertical integration	1.800	2.474	3.349	4.158	9.61***
Horizontal integration	1.700	2.778	3.214	3.868	11.17***
Buyers/sellers	2.600	3.737	3.744	5.447	15.29***
INT'L EXTERNAL INTEGRATION					
External mktg agreements	2.000	3.579	3.805	4.027	3.76**
External R&D agreements	2.100	2.316	3.024	4.105	7.71***
Production sharing	1.500	4.211	3.605	4.973	15.99***
Information networks	1.700	4.105	3.976	4.821	12.46***

a* Significance of difference in strategy means, $p < 0.10$
** Significance of difference in strategy means, $p < 0.05$
*** Significance of difference in strategy means, $p < 0.001$

Cluster 1: Domestic, Product Specialization Strategy. Business competing in Cluster 1 can best be described as competing with domestically oriented, product specialization strategies. While Cluster 1 businesses placed a strong emphasis on manufacturing prowess, quality reputation, and marketing prowess, what distinguished businesses in this cluster was their comparatively high emphasis on product specialization. As shown in

Figure 4.6, this resulted from the highest emphasis being placed on the "emphasizing specialty products" strategy variable (5.091) than on any of the other three clusters. Manufacturing specialty products would also suggest the importance that manufacturing prowess plays in defining strategic behavior. In this cluster, variables associated with manufacturing prowess were particularly important, including "promoting innovative manufacturing" (5.818), "emphasizing modern plant and equipment" (5.545), and "developing efficient manufacturing process" (6.000).

Figure 4.7
Comparison of Mean Levels of International Activity among Four-Cluster Solution[a]

CLUSTER	TOTAL SALES ($M)	CLUSTER	INT'L SALES ($M)
4	1119.9	3	443.6
3	918.5	2	431.0
2	790.1	4	291.7
1	516.4	1	54.1

CLUSTER	INTERNATIONAL AS % OF TOTAL SALES	CLUSTER	NO. OF COUNTRIES
3	38.88	4	14.09
4	37.15	3	10.26
2	31.49	2	3.00
1	16.05	1	1.20

CLUSTER	FOREIGN OPERATING PROFIT (%)	CLUSTER	FOREIGN ASSETS (%)
4	33.79	4	24.00
3	32.64	3	19.12
2	23.50	1	10.00
1	8.60	2	6.75

Note: means covered by the same line are not significantly different

[a]significant at the $p > 0.10$ level

Businesses located in Cluster 1 were also the most domestically oriented of business in any of the four clusters. Little emphasis was placed on the four international strategic factors. This is evidenced in Figure 4.6 where in every instance Cluster 1 businesses placed the least emphasis on international investment, political, and internal and external variables. With regard to the levels of international activity shown in Figure 4.7, businesses in Cluster 1 competed in significantly fewer countries and had significantly lower percentage levels of both foreign operating profits and foreign assets than businesses in Clusters 3 and 4. Also, while not statistically significant, Cluster 1 businesses showed lower levels of international sales as a percentage of total sales (16.05 percent) of businesses than any other cluster. This is again consistent with a group of domestically oriented businesses.

Cluster 2: Exporting, High-Quality Offerings Strategy. Cluster 2 businesses seem to be pursuing strategies based on exporting high-quality offerings in terms of both products and services. This pattern of strategic behavior is shown by a high positive mean for the quality reputation strategic factor and a strong emphasis on all four international strategic factors, particularly the international political dimension. Yet, as is apparent in Figure 4.7, Cluster 2 businesses have the lowest levels of foreign assets as a percentage of total assets of four clusters. This, coupled with the high levels of international sales to total sales (31.49 percent), indicates a clear emphasis on accessing international markets through exports. Cluster 2 businesses also limited direct investments to relatively few countries (Figure 4.7), indicating that exports were focused on only a few key markets. The high cluster mean for the international political strategic factor (Figure 4.5) suggests a strong disposition both to lobby foreign governments and to seek out U.S. government assistance in penetrating foreign markets (Figure 4.6).

Cluster 2 businesses also place a considerable emphasis on the quality reputation strategic factor seen in Figure 4.5. Here, the emphasis on quality is supported by the strong mean response for the variable associated with the importance of a positive industry reputation (Figure 4.6). The cluster is also noted for low emphasis on manufacturing prowess. This results from a low emphasis on both "capacity utilization" and "modern plant and equipment" (Figure 4.6). The product specialization factor is also the lowest of the four clusters, underscoring that products associated with this cluster are more mainstream in demand. In addition, this cluster is noted for a negative mean factor score for the prestige products strategic factor (–0.415), seen in Figure 4.5. While much of this is the result of an emphasis on tightly controlling costs (Figure 4.6), the significance of mean cluster responses to this variable is only $p > 0.10$. Rather, the negative mean for the high-price factor is much more significantly attributable to a low emphasis on high-price products, reflective of the extent of price competition for high-quality mainstream products.

Cluster 3: International, Product Innovation Strategy. Businesses grouped in Cluster 3 can be described as pursuing an international strategy focusing on product innovation. Here, the businesses are identified by a high emphasis on quality reputation, marketing prowess, manufacturing prowess, and the four international strategic factors including international investment, political, and internal and external integration strategic factors. Yet compared with Clusters 1, 2, and 4, Cluster 3 businesses place particularly high emphasis on the prestige products factor. This is also evidenced by the highest cluster mean for the variable "producing high-priced products for market niches" and the lowest cluster mean for "pricing at or below competitive price levels," both shown in Figure 4.6. Innovative products are most often associated with premium pricing. When compared with businesses in the other clusters, Cluster 3 businesses also strongly emphasized product specialization. Again, this is consistent with producing innovative products for a variety of international customers.

Although Cluster 3 businesses strongly emphasized the variable associated with the promotion of new product development, no significant differences separated businesses in the four clusters along this dimension. It should be emphasized, however, that promoting new product development does not necessarily equate with promoting innovative products. Clarification of the content of the product innovation strategies of member businesses is provided in the posttest.

Businesses contained in Cluster 3 also strongly emphasized all four of the international strategic factors. However, Cluster 3 businesses did not seem to support the international investment, international political, international internal integration, and international external integration strategic factors to the same extent as Cluster 4 businesses. While the levels themselves are important, Cluster 3 businesses did not compete in as much of a globally consistent manner as Cluster 4 businesses. Rather, Cluster 3 businesses exhibited patterns of strategic behavior that appeared to be much more internationally than globally oriented. Businesses in Cluster 3 maintained subsidiaries or joint ventures in significantly more countries than either Cluster 2 or Cluster 1 businesses. Also, although no significant differences existed between the clusters in terms of international sales levels, Cluster 3 businesses showed the highest overall level of international sales. Although not significantly different at the 0.10 level from Clusters 2 and 4, Cluster 3 businesses also displayed the highest ratio of international sales to total sales (38.88 percent) of the four clusters. This will be more fully discussed in Chapter 5. Cluster 3 businesses also earned a significantly higher level of operating profits from overseas operations than businesses in Cluster 1, and while not statistically significant at the 0.10 level, Cluster 3 businesses had higher levels of foreign assets as a percentage of total assets than businesses in Clusters 1 and 2. This is indicative of a group of businesses pursuing highly international, but not necessarily global, business strategies.

Cluster 4: Global, Combination Strategy. Of all the businesses competing in the global industries, businesses in Cluster 4 appear to demonstrate what the literature has frequently described as traditional global strategies. This includes highest cluster means on the international investment, international political, international internal integration, and international external integration strategic factors. Cluster 4 businesses also maintained subsidiaries or joint ventures in the most number of countries, had the highest level of total sales, had the highest levels of foreign operating profits as a percentage of total profits, and had the highest levels of foreign assets to total assets of businesses from any of the other clusters.

What this represents is a group of businesses that are highly integrated on a global basis, with value activities spread around the world, acting with high levels of political awareness and skills and operating with high degrees of international investment acumen. These conclusions are also supported in Figure 4.6, where cluster means associated with each of the international strategy variables are consistently and significantly the highest for Cluster 4 businesses. Yet with all this international activity, there is no evidence that Cluster 4 businesses are ambivalent with respect to competing in either home or host countries. Indeed, for the businesses in this cluster, international sales to total sales (37.15 percent) were slightly—although not significantly—lower than levels displayed by businesses in the "international product innovation" cluster. This may raise questions about the extent to which Cluster 4 businesses emphasize truly global strategies.

In competitive positioning, Cluster 4 businesses appear to place a very strong emphasis on both manufacturing prowess and marketing prowess. More particularly, Cluster 4 businesses placed significantly more emphasis on the variables associated with "capacity utilization" and "manufacturing efficiency" than businesses in the other three clusters. Similarly, with respect to marketing prowess, Cluster 4 businesses more strongly emphasized "monitoring market opportunities," "controlling distribution channels," and "developing innovative marketing techniques" than businesses in the other three clusters. This seems to indicate a combination strategy where businesses concurrently emphasize both manufacturing abilities and marketing skills. The pursuance of combination competitive positioning strategies has not been advanced in the strategic management literature either in solely domestic or global industry contexts.

PERFORMANCE MEASURES

Objective performance measures were used to assess the relative success of businesses in each of the four clusters. These measures included three-year average return on assets, three-year average return on investment, and three-year average annual increase in total sales. Performance means are presented in Figure 4.8. Also reported are comparisons between cluster means using the Duncan multiple-range procedure. This procedure

Figure 4.8
Comparison of Performance Means among Four-Cluster Solution

PERFORMANCE MEANS[a]

CLUSTER	ROA[b]	CLUSTER	ROI[c]	CLUSTER	SALES GROWTH[c]
4	4.188	3	4.114	3	4.378
3	4.514	4	4.267	4	4.571
2	4.737	2	4.611	1	5.125
1	5.571	1	5.333	2	5.368

Note: means covered by the same line are not significantly different

[a]clusters are ranked according to performance, with-the highest-performing clusters listed first, the lowest performing clusters listed last. Results are reported using a scale ranging from 1 to 7.

[b]Return on Assets - significant at the $p > 0.05$ level

[c]Return on Investment - significant at the $p > 0.10$ level

tests for differences between all means. A further discussion of the relationship between the four-cluster strategies and performance is found in Chapter 6.

SUMMARY OF THE EMPIRICAL CLASSIFICATION

This chapter has provided the data analysis necessary for the development of an empirical taxonomy of business strategies in global industries. The sample contained 115 businesses representing 11 different global industries. After testing for outliers, three businesses were removed from the sample.

Four separate strategy constructs were operationalized through a total of 35 different competitive strategy variables. From this, five competitive

Figure 4.9
Empirical Classification Findings

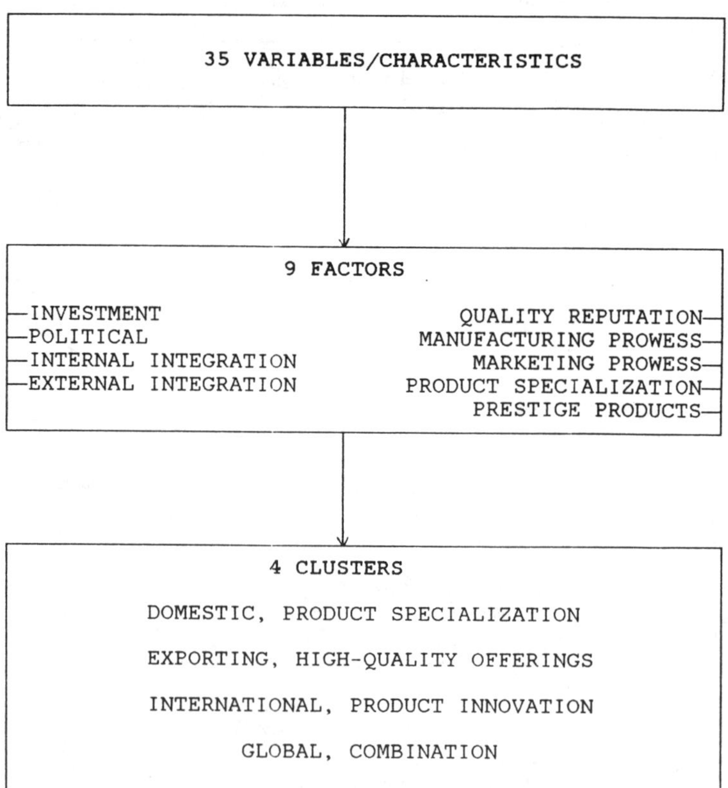

positioning factors were identified: quality reputation, manufacturing prowess, marketing prowess, innovative products, and high-price niche. In addition, international political, international investment, and international internal and external integration factors were identified. Factor scores were then clustered and a four-cluster solution selected. The four cluster strategies were identified as (1) domestic, product specialization, (2) exporting, high-quality offerings, (3) international, innovative products, and (4) global, combination. Performance means and levels of international activity were also reported for each cluster. Figure 4.9 presents a summary of the empirical classification findings.

ADDITIONAL MEASURES OF BUSINESS STRATEGIES

While cluster analysis provides an extremely useful classification tool, definitive conclusions cannot be drawn exclusively from the process. As a consequence, in this study, a combination of two different qualitative methods was used to substantiate the derived classification. These include the use of secondary data sources and posttest interviews. Each of these will now be discussed in more detail.

Secondary Data Sources

Secondary data, provided by annual reports, internal company literature, and industry publications, were gathered for 17 businesses representing each of the four clusters. An attempt was made to increase the number of businesses covered, but several problems emerged in doing this. In many cases the companies were private and annual reports were not available. In other cases the annual reports either focused exclusively on corporate-level strategy or addressed business-level strategy in such a peripheral manner as to make interpretation of relevant business strategies extremely problematic. As a result, caution should be exercised in generalizing from the limited number of businesses with available secondary strategy data to entire groups of businesses associated with the empirically derived clusters.

Cluster 1 businesses demonstrated market orientations that were very domestic in nature. Secondary data from three businesses representing three distinct SIC code industries (SIC 2879, SIC 3552, SIC 3724) were reviewed. These businesses all produced specialized products for market niches. Products were all high quality. Sales were almost exclusively based in the United States. In one case, a small but growing percentage of sales was being generated by exports to one country. Although international sales volumes were small, all the businesses had explicit objectives of increasing international sales through exports. Overall, there was strong confirmation of the appropriateness of labeling the strategic behavior of Cluster 1 businesses as being domestically oriented with an emphasis on product specialization.

The secondary data for Cluster 2 businesses contained information from four separate businesses. However, only two different SIC code industries were represented (SIC 3533 and SIC 3721). In this group of businesses, exports through overseas sales offices were the norm. Also, Cluster 2 businesses placed far less emphasis on developing innovative products than was evidenced with Cluster 3 businesses. Rather, a strong emphasis was placed on producing high-quality products with long product lives. Quality was the most often cited basis of competitive strategy among these four businesses. In one instance, coproduction agreements had been established with partners in Indonesia, Japan, Norway, and Turkey. However, in this case, as in the cases of the three remaining businesses examined, the bulk of production clearly remained in the United States.

The secondary data for Cluster 3 businesses contained information from five separate businesses, each representative of different SIC code industries (SIC 2879, SIC 3532, SIC 3651, SIC 3721, and SIC 3728). These businesses all stressed state-of-the-art, high-tech products. Within their respective SIC industries, competitive advantage was achieved when businesses produced a broad array of innovative products. In addition to relying on product innovation, several standardized products were also offered.

Cluster 3 businesses placed a strong emphasis on accessing international markets through a combination of exports and various forms of overseas joint ventures. Market perspective was international but not global. For example, according to one senior executive from a civil helicopter manufacturer: "We have only in the last few years begun to think of the rest of the world as a business area and not just a market."[36] Production, while generally U.S. based, sometimes consisted of overseas final assembly operations, typically for political purposes. Overseas sales offices were common. Distribution coalitions were commonly used; risk-sharing coalitions were also prominently used for high-tech product development. In this group of five businesses, product design always originated in the United States. In all, there was a strong confirmation of the international, innovative products strategy suggested through the empirical procedures.

Cluster 4 businesses demonstrated patterns of strategic behavior most clearly associated with global business strategies. Secondary data from five businesses representing four different SIC code industries (SIC 2879, SIC 3721, SIC 3724, and SIC 3728) were reviewed. In these businesses, heavy emphasis was placed on the configuring of particularly downstream value activities around the world. International strategic coalitions were selectively utilized for assembly and product distribution. Even without coalitions, overseas assembly of finished products was common. Foreign government-controlled agencies were often a party to these coalitions, thus underscoring the importance of international political activities.

With regard to the nature of the empirically identified combination competitive positioning strategies, evidence suggested that manufacturing prowess was geared not so much to supporting an overall low-cost strategy as it was to supporting a strategy based on a complex innovation strategy geared to producing high-technology products efficiently. To this end, the complex innovation strategy was quite similar to the Cluster 3 competitive positioning strategy of product innovation. However, two important differences separated the complex innovation strategy of Cluster 3 businesses and the high-technology strategy of Cluster 4 businesses. The first difference was the *breadth* of technological innovation that characterized the product line offered by Cluster 4 businesses. Unlike Cluster 3 businesses that offered some standardized products, Cluster 4 business competed exclusively on the basis of producing a stream of highly innovative products. The second difference was the *depth* of technological innovation that characterized Cluster 4 businesses. Cluster 4 businesses relied regularly and heavily on massive commitments of R&D investments. In contrast, the innovative products strategy of Cluster 3 businesses does not necessarily demand huge commitments of high-technology R&D resources.

The second leg of the combination competitive positioning strategy, marketing prowess, was focused on differentiating products according to this high-technology position. Industry reputation for technological prowess was particularly stressed. Price competition was generally of secondary concern.

Posttest Interviews

Along with reviewing secondary data, posttests interviews were conducted to ascertain the convergent validity of the classification and provide a richer description of each strategy group. In order to minimize potential bias, at least two businesses from each cluster were involved in each stage of the posttest. Furthermore, businesses from each cluster had to be members of different SIC code industries. Beyond this, no prior knowledge existed of the strategies of the businesses selected. Finally, an attempt was made to select a geographically disperse group of businesses in order to minimize potential regional bias in strategic behavior. Even given these precautions, care should be exercised in generalizing from the limited number of businesses interviewed to entire groups of businesses associated with the empirically derived strategy clusters.

In all, interviews were conducted with executives from nine different businesses representing seven separate SIC code industries. Interviews were held with divisional presidents or top executives responsible for determining the strategic behavior of the identified business units. Interviews were conducted at head offices in Connecticut, New Jersey, North Carolina, South Carolina, and California. Average time spent in each interview was from one to one and a half hours. During this time, prepared, open-ended questions were asked about each business's actions according to previously identified strategic factors. A summary of the posttest findings for each of the four strategy groups is included below.

Domestic, Product Specialization Strategy Group. In the posttest, executives from two businesses representing the "domestic, product specialization" strategy were interviewed. The first business competed in the mining machinery industry (SIC 3532); the second business competed in the synthetic fungicides and pesticides industry (SIC 2879). Both businesses concentrated heavily on domestic sales: foreign sales accounted for very little of the total sales in either business. Beyond the preoccupation with domestic competition, the following summary comments are provided.

1. *Production of specialty mature products stressed.* Both businesses strongly supported a narrow product line focused on specialty products that larger competitors could not or would not produce. In the case of the mining machinery manufacturer, emphasis was on manufacturing a "narrower group of products" than key competitors. Products were typically mature, having generally been abandoned by competitors as they moved on to newer, higher-technology offerings. By focusing on a limited number of products, businesses could develop manufacturing and marketing expertise unsurpassed by competitors. Quality was an important objective in product manufacture. However, given the limited potential economies of scale, manufacturers were never to pursue low-cost strategies fully.

2. *Intention to increase sales through exports.* Businesses were overwhelmingly interested in export markets as a future avenue to increase

total sales. Licensing was viewed as a weak alternative, given high levels of technology standardization. In the case of the mining machinery manufacturer, international sales already represented about 15 percent of total sales. Much of these sales came from a small overseas parts facility (in Scotland) that had been acquired from a licensee at fire-sale prices. Parts produced were shipped back to the business's plants in the United States to be incorporated as components in one of the business's finished products. No plan or intent existed to build another overseas facility. Indeed, concern over control issues raised serious questions over the long-term viability of this present European operation. Rather, the business had made an explicit objective of increasing international sales through exports from the United States. The low value of the U.S. dollar in the late 1980s was viewed as an encouragement to higher international sales.

Exporting, High-Quality Offerings Strategy Group. Executives from two businesses representing two SIC code industries (SIC 3552, textile machinery; and SIC 3651, radio receiving equipment—with an emphasis on microwave reception apparatus) were interviewed in the posttest. The following findings summarize and help clarify the identification of the "exporting, high-quality offerings" strategy group.

1. *Products are based on standardized mature technology.* The businesses interviewed in the "exporting, high-quality offerings" strategy group emphasized products based on standardized, mature technology. The textile machinery manufacturer, for example, produced looms based on technology over ten years old. Few patents were still in force. By relying on standardized product technology, however, the business could be assured of homogenous product demand virtually anywhere in the world. This same emphasis on mature technology was also reported by the microwave receiver business, which relied on technology that was also at least ten years old.

2. *Strong emphasis on high-quality offerings*. The importance of providing high-quality products and services was universally supported by the businesses interviewed in this strategy group. For the textile machinery manufacturer, for example, quality was a key factor in making sales both at home and abroad. Price was of only secondary importance to customers, who often ran looms 24 hours a day, 365 days a year. Reliability, which was most clearly associated with quality, reduced critical downtime. In this case, reliability was facilitated through the use of standardized technology. Other competitors that focused on premium-priced technology—for example, manufacturers who combined water jet weaving technology with sophisticated electronic controls—could charge premium pricing but

could not deliver the same degree of reliability. The microwave receiver business also strongly stressed high-quality offerings. One indication of this commitment to quality was the business's warranty, which extended for two years instead of the industry norm of one year. According to an executive in this business, "Quality is key because our customers are so far away." This was particularly true for purchasers of portable microwave reception equipment, which was often used in developing countries, far away from both the supplier in the United States and service representatives in Europe or Japan.

Service quality was also judged to be a critical dimension of the strategies of group 2 businesses. The textile machinery manufacturer, for example, suggested that its "parts service is the best in the industry." Attention to technical support, parts replacements, and training was regarded as critical to the continued success of the businesses interviewed. The microwave receiver business also strongly stressed service quality. According to one top executive, "Product quality is important, but you have to have support" in terms of service facilities, parts, and project financing.

3. *International activities dominated by exports*. While domestic operations were critically important to the vitality of the businesses in group 2, international sales also played an essential role in determining performance. International sales were, in turn, dominated by exports. The microwave receiver business, for example, relied on exports for half of its sales volume. The cash flow provided by export sales was essential for ongoing R&D.

The importance of export sales in the maintenance of even low-level R&D projects is best illustrated with the textile machinery manufacturer. With the rising U.S. dollar in the early 1980s, this business lost virtually all foreign sales. Because of rising imports, domestic sales were also hurt. Major cuts in product and process R&D have followed. Now only replacement parts are exported. And although the dollar has fallen in value during the latter half of the 1980s, the business's international distribution channels, devastated in the first half of the decade, have proved difficult to rebuild. Without exports, the business's future looks bleak.

4. *Preoccupation with, but little reliance on, government assistance programs*. Government export assistance was cited in the survey as critically important in penetrating foreign markets. In the posttest interviews, there almost seemed to be a preoccupation with government assistance—whether positive or negative. However, even given the high profile of government assistance, the government was not viewed as

playing a significant role in increasing overall export levels. Rather, managers felt that the advantages of export assistance were not commensurate with investment in time required to secure government help. The government was also viewed as an unreliable and fickle partner.

International, Product Innovation Strategy Group. Executives from three businesses representing the international, product innovation group were interviewed in the posttest. The businesses represented large divisions in *Fortune* 100 corporations. Of the businesses, the first competed in the civil aircraft industry (SIC 3721) by producing civil helicopters, the second business competed in the synthetic fungicides and insecticides industry (SIC 2879), and the third business competed in the aircraft parts industry (SIC 3728). The following findings assist in summarizing and clarifying the broad dimensions of strategic behavior for the global combination strategy group.

1. *Internationally standardized innovative products.* Without exception, the businesses studied all sold a broad array of internationally standardized products. Only minor cosmetic changes were made to meet local market demand. Effectively the same product sold in Singapore would be sold in Paris or Buenos Aires. The products were also innovative in nature. For example, according to a senior executive of the agricultural chemical business unit, "Product innovation gets you the business." While product innovation is critical, the core technology remained fairly constant across the businesses. R&D activities were more applied. Consequently, business unit technological changes seemed less pervasive or deep-seated than evident in the complex innovation strategy pursued by global competitors.

By basing product innovation more on "bells and whistles" than on central product technology, the extent of product innovation across a broad array of products generally far exceeded those of competitors. For example, the helicopter manufacturer sold a wider line of final products than any other helicopter manufacturer in the industry. Product innovation was geared to providing styling and performance modifications to base helicopter platforms developed for the U.S. military. Similarly, the agricultural chemical manufacturer focused on developing "newer, safer, and higher-performing products" by tapping into the research acumen of sister business units. This typically involved sharing R&D facilities and production plants. The aircraft parts business also stressed a broad line of high-tech components. With this business, however, far fewer intracorporate technology transfers typically took place.

2. *Premium pricing.* By focusing differentiation on product innovation, businesses could command premium prices for their products. Products

represented top-of-the-line offerings in the industry. For example, the helicopter manufacturer sold fewer units but had significantly higher revenues than its chief rival. According to a senior executive in this business unit: "Quality is far more important than price." Similarly, by focusing on producing the highest-performing products, both the agricultural chemicals business and the aircraft parts business were able to demand constantly top prices for their products based on price/performance assessments made by customers.

Another aspect of emphasizing premium pricing was that much of the value added was achieved at the point of final product sale. For example, the aircraft parts business maintained a large marketing/sales/final-assembly facility in Toulouse, France, in order to remain close to the AirBus consortium. Across the businesses in this strategy group, it was essential that control be maintained over final customer sales. This was essential, not for initial customer sales but just as importantly to guarantee the quality of after-sales service demanded by customers. In the case of the agricultural chemical manufacturer, for example, about 80 percent of U.S. export sales were handled through brokers. These brokers, in turn, handled the international distribution of the products, eventually reselling many of them to overseas sales offices of the original business unit.

3. *Reactionary international strategy.* The businesses studied seemed to approach the international configuration of business activities in an ad hoc, case-by-case manner. The bulk of total business unit output was geared to meeting U.S. demand. Exports were used to supply some, but by no means all, of the overseas demand. Remaining demand was met through a combination of licensing arrangements and production-sharing joint ventures. Licensees typically received exclusive rights for their own country and were allowed access via exports to certain foreign markets. In contrast, joint ventures were aimed at either national markets or, in some instances, regional markets.

Several reasons were cited for using coalitions. Licensing arrangements were typically designed to penetrate key foreign markets closed for political reasons to foreign direct investment. International joint ventures were established principally to provide improved access to international markets, either through appeasing national governments or accessing local market penetration skills. The aircraft parts business, for example, relied heavily on local agents in attempting to influence host nation political figures. International suppliers, both for U.S. facilities and non-U.S. plants, were almost without exception selected for reasons of political expediency.

Global, Combination Strategy Group. Executives from three businesses representing the global, combination strategy group were interviewed in the posttest. The businesses were all large divisions of *Fortune* 100 corporations. Of the three businesses, one competed in the semiconductor industry (SIC 3674), the second business competed in the aircraft parts industry (SIC 3728), concentrating on the manufacture of civil aircraft engines; and the third business competed in the fungicide and pesticide industry (SIC 2879). The following findings assist in summarizing and clarifying the broad dimensions of strategic behavior for the global combination strategy group.

1. *Core skills/activities are located in the United States.* Upstream activities for all three businesses were located exclusively in the United States. Chief among these activities were R&D/technological development and the manufacturing of key components. In the case of the manufacturer of aircraft engines, for example, core engineering and product design skills were simply unavailable overseas. While for the semiconductor manufacturer these requisite skills were available overseas, close relationships with other corporate divisions mandated a centralization of R&D and technological development activitites. In the case of the pesticide manufacturer, corporate headquarters had assigned world product mandates for insecticides, fungicides, and herbicides to divisions in the United States, France, and England, respectively. In the United States example, basic research, key product development work, and initial product formulation were all carried out domestically. All three SIC code businesses felt threatened with the potential loss of proprietary technologies if these central activities were transferred to overseas locations.

2. *Downstream activities located in overseas locations.* Production and assembly operations were dispersed throughout the world. Three primary reasons were cited for this phenomenon, including (1) the need to establish a permanent presence in key national/regional markets, (2) host government pressures for foreign direct investment, and (3) the desire to access low-cost labor. The semiconductor manufacturer perceived that all three factors acted in concert to determine the location and nature of the foreign investment decisions. With the aircraft engine business, motivation for the heavy reliance on the globalization of downstream activities was principally a combination of both political pressures and market presence factors—particularly in the repair segment of the market. So pervasive were the political pressures—largely in terms of offset trade demands—that the aircraft engine business unit faced that it had developed significant countertrading abilities. These same skills had not yet been required of the

semiconductor business unit, although it was predicted that the day of their use was fast approaching. In the case of the pesticide manufacturer some formulation (final mixing of the chemical ingredients) was carried out locally in Argentina, Brazil, Indonesia, and South Africa. However, these overseas facilities were not established because of potential gains due to certain economies but because of intense local political pressures.

3. *Reliance on coalitions.* Three reasons were commonly cited for establishing international coalitions: (1) host nation law mandated local partnerships; (2) local partners could provide capital for the investment; and (3) local partners had marketing and/or political skills requisite to conduct business in the host nation effectively (for example, the pesticide business unit relied heavily on product distribution coalitions to assist in market penetration). No instances existed where coalitions were used for pure research purposes. More common were product development coalitions involving other industry competitors. Only minor input geared to making "cosmetic" product changes were provided by local customers. However, coalitions were regularly used for the manufacture and assembly of finished products. A major challenge with the establishment of the coalition was the prevention of key technology transfers (largely related to design and production processes) to coalition partners.

4. *Combination strategies—complex innovation and marketing differentiation.* The posttests confirmed a strong reliance on a combination complex innovation and marketing differentiation strategy. Complex innovation relates to an integrated effort—involving both the business unit and related businesses within the corporate framework—extending to all aspects of value activities. For example, within a parent corporation that prides itself on its technological prowess, the semiconductor business unit also plays a key role in determining overall corporate effectiveness. The semiconductor business has a strong, technology-driven symbiotic relationship with other business units within the corporation.

Within the business unit, complex innovation permeated the entire value chain. High-tech R&D, highly complex product design, and specific high-value-added production processes resulted in streams of complex state-of-the-art products coming to market. The semiconductor business unit, for example, targeted two related markets: in-house systems buyers and custom and semicustom external buyers. By focusing on these buyers, one senior international executive asserted, "High-tech product innovation is absolutely critical in order to compete." For this very reason, the business unit employed several Nobel Prize–winning physicists in its research facilities. In a similar manner, a senior executive in the aircraft engine business unit argued that product innovation is "absolutely the key to long-term competitiveness."

Given the high degree of product standardization across national markets, marketing differentiation was focused on building industry reputation for technology, quality, reliability, and permanence in given host markets. To illustrate, the pesticide manufacturer relied heavily on a "push" marketing strategy aimed at moving products through distributors and a "pull" strategy aimed at inciting demand through the product's ultimate consumers, the world's farmers. The message to both groups was the same: quality, reliability, and the unique technical features of the product.

While competitors had large market shares with broad ranges of products, businesses expressed concern over customer perceptions that they lacked a permanent commitment to a given host market. This is an important facet in winning initial sales because the highly technological nature of the products mandates high levels of before- and after-sales service indicating that the customer wants some assurance that the business is committed to the market for the long run. According to the aircraft engine manufacturer: "After-sales service is at least as important as actual product quality in making the sale." The importance of service led businesses to integrate downstream in order to control channels of distribution more fully. Again, this was not so much a function of desire for cost efficiency as an expressed need to maintain control over before- and after-sales service.

Given the importance of product innovation, service, and quality, it is not surprising that buyers were generally price insensitive. Products were not mass-market items. Sales generally took years to arrange and involved large orders. Although producing in an efficient a manner as possible, competitors in this group regarded price as a "secondary concern to buyers." Customers seemed willing to pay for a "package" that included both product and service.

5. *Lack of a fully global market perspective.* While the businesses interviewed expressed a deep interest in international markets, it was clearly evident that an especially strong commitment existed to the home U.S. marketplace. In no instance did a business unit consider itself unbiased in its market orientation. Competitive success in the United States was preeminently important. While component and finished product flow typically crossed several national and regional borders, the scope of market share battles outside the United States were regional. Executives argued that the provincial, ethnocentric perspectives of middle and top managers

constituted a critical obstacle in developing a more global perspective for the business unit.

In addition to a preoccupation with U.S. market position, international business strategy was formulated with a regional perspective of competition. For example, in the case of the pesticide manufacturer, the world was broken into regions including Europe, North America, South America, and the Pacific Rim. Other competitors, while stronger or weaker in a particular area, had also divided the world into similar regions. By a "gentleman's agreement" between top executives of worldwide competitors, competitive battles were contained within these regions. Within the regions, regional headquarters managers initiated market share battles, whether involving price or marketing actions. While the world headquarters knew and approved of these actions, efforts were made to limit confrontation to single regions. The ultimate objective was to maximize profits while maintaining good relationships among competitors. This private and informal association of top global managers from competing businesses was warmly referred to as the "club." Thus, while competitors were global in many regards, market share battles were not.

SUMMARY

In this chapter three different methodological tools were employed in developing a classification of business strategies in global industries. These include survey data collection, secondary data collection, and in-depth interviews. With the use of survey data, several multivariate data reduction techniques were employed to develop an initial four-cluster solution. These procedures included principal components analysis, cluster analysis, ANOVA, and chi-square tests. Secondary data involving 17 different businesses and posttest interviews conducted with executives from nine different businesses were then utilized to both confirm and extend the classification. Here it was recognized that empirical analysis alone represents only the first cut of a more complete business strategy classification.

By using these three different methodological tools, four composite strategies in global industries were identified: "domestic, product specialization," "exporting, high-quality offerings," "international, product innovation," and "global, combination" with an emphasis on complex innovation and marketing differentiation. Each of these composite strategies is based on a combination of competitive positioning and internationalization strategy dimensions.

In the development of this classification of business strategies, various levels of analysis have been used. The use of lower-level components in developing a more abstract classification is strongly supported in the literature.[37] The strategy classification terminology consistent with these four levels of abstraction include: (1) *characteristics*, representing business unit response to 35 different strategies; (2) *factors*, representing nine different patterns of strategy characteristics; (3) *types*, composed of eight broader patterns of strategic behavior bounded by two discrete strategy *dimensions* (competitive positioning and internationalization); and (4) taxa

Figure 4.10
Hierarchical Nature of the Strategy Classification

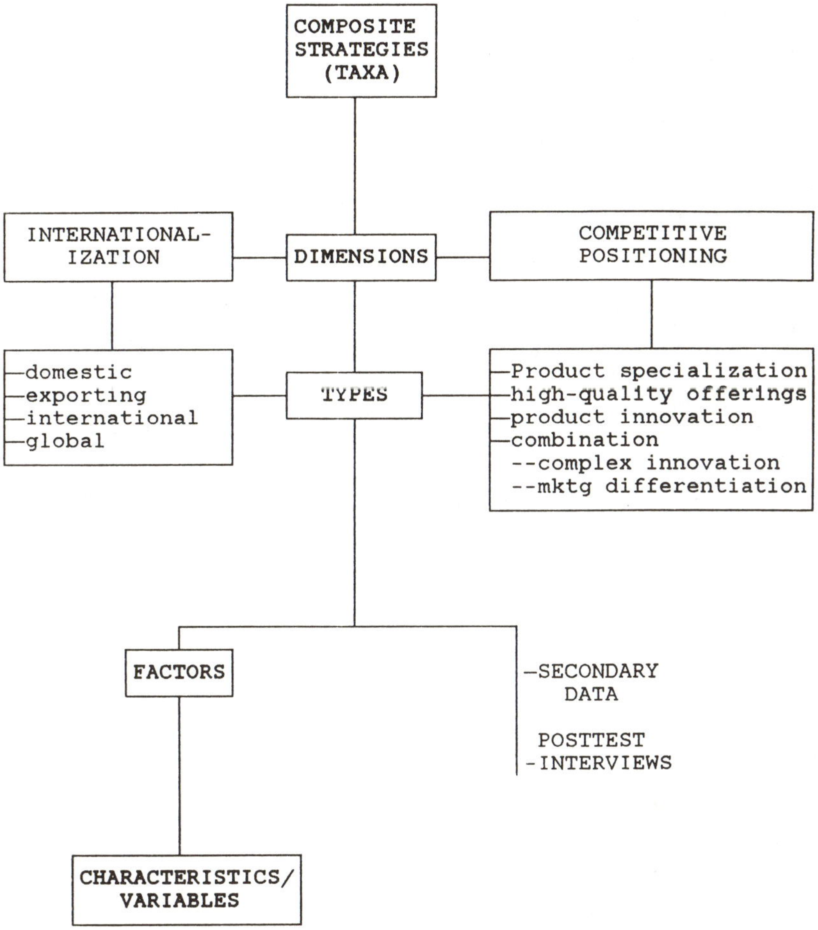

or composite strategies, reflective of patterns among strategy dimensions. The terminology that reflects the relationships between and roots of these four different levels of classification attributes is reviewed in Figure 4.10.

The interaction of internationalization and competitive positioning dimensions in determining composite business strategies is more fully discussed in Chapter 5. Chapter 6 explores the relationship between each of the four composite strategies in global industries and perceptions that businesses have of pressures that determine the extent of industry globalness.

NOTES

1. Pfaffenberger and Patterson (1981).
2. Ibid. and Netter, Waserman, and Kutner (1985).
3. Dillon and Goldstein (1984: 24).
4. C. Galbraith and Schendel (1983), White (1986), Douglas and Rhee (1987), and Miller (1987a).
5. Jackson (1980: 205).
6. Dillon and Goldstein (1984).
7. Hair, Anderson, and Tatham (1987: 243).
8. Kim and Mueller (1978), Dillon and Goldstein (1984), and Hair, Anderson, and Tatham (1987).
9. Kim and Mueller (1978) and Dillon and Goldstein (1984).
10. D. Morrison (1967) and C. Galbraith and Schendel (1983).
11. Green, Frank, and Robinson (1967).
12. Kim and Mueller (1978), Stewart (1981), Dillon and Goldstein (1984), and Hair, Anderson, and Tatham (1987).
13. Hair, Anderson, and Tatham (1987: 247).
14. Cattell (1966), Kim and Mueller (1978), Stewart (1981), and Hair, Anderson, and Tatham (1987).
15. See Miller and Friesen (1978), Dess and Davis (1984), Robinson and Pearce (1985), Davis (1986), and D. Morrison (1967).
16. Kim and Mueller (1978).
17. Punj and Stewart (1983: 135).
18. Green, Frank, and Robinson (1967).
19. Hair, Anderson, and Tatham (1987).
20. Gale (1972).
21. Hatten (1979), C. Galbraith and Schendel (1983), Hambrick (1983b), Dess and Davis (1984), Harrigan (1985a), Davis (1986), Smith and Grimm (1987), and Robinson and Pearce (1988).
22. Hambrick (1983a) and Prescott (1983).
23. Hair, Anderson, and Tatham (1987).
24. Ibid., p. 260.
25. Dillon and Goldstein (1984).
26. Punj and Stewart (1983: 143–144).

27. Dillon and Goldstein (1984: 186).

28. Hartigan (1975), Milligan (1980), and Punj and Stewart (1983).

29. While principal components analysis has been noted for its robustness (Dillon and Goldstein, 1984), the factor loadings shown in Figures 4.1 to 4.4 reflect the elimination of these three outliers.

30. For a discussion of cluster identification, see Hartigan (1975), Punj and Stewart (1983), Aldenderfer and Blashfield (1984), and Hair, Anderson, and Tatham (1987).

31. This point is made by Green, Frank, and Robinson (1967), Hambrick (1984), and Harrigan (1985a).

32. Lehmann (1979).

33. Sarle (1983), Hambrick (1984), Aldenderfer and Blashfield (1984), Harrigan (1985a), and Hair, Anderson, and Tatham (1987).

34. Lehmann (1979).

35. Sarle (1983).

36. D. Lawrence (1988: 12).

37. Sneath and Sokal (1973), McKelvey (1982), and Chrisman, Hofer, and Boulton (1988).

CHAPTER 5

GLOBAL INDUSTRY STRATEGY CLASSIFICATION: SOME THEORETICAL EXTENSIONS

The purpose of this chapter is to discuss more fully the business strategy classification in global industries that was identified in Chapter 4. The chapter is divided into three major sections. The first section provides an overview of the derived strategy classification. Here the roles of strategy types and dimensions are discussed in relation to the formulation of composite strategies or strategy taxa. The second section addresses the role the internationalization dimension plays in providing the building blocks for the strategy classification. In this section each of the four internationalization strategy types identified in Chapter 4 (domestic, exporting, international, and global) are more fully discussed within the context of existing literature. The third section of the chapter addresses the role the competitive positioning dimension plays in determining the strategy classification. In this section, competitive positioning strategy types (product specialization, high-quality offerings, product innovation, and combination) are discussed within the context of existing literature. The final section of the chapter discusses how internationalization and competitive positioning interact to produce strategy taxa or composite strategies. The relationship between internationalization and competitive positioning is more fully explored using the integration/responsiveness framework developed by Prahalad and Doz.[1]

COMPOSITE STRATEGIES: THE IMPORTANCE OF STRATEGY DIMENSIONS

The use of multiple methodological tools has resulted in the identification of four composite strategies in global industries. These include (1) "domestic, product specialization," (2) "exporting, high-quality offerings," (3) "international, product innovation," and (4) "global, combination" strategies. These identified patterns suggest that businesses competing in global industries pursue more complex strategies than previously posited.

In identifying strategy taxa or composite strategies, two broad strategy dimensions were isolated: internationalization and competitive positioning. Within each of these two dimensions, four different strategy types were observed. This hierarchical classification of business strategies in global industries is reviewed in Figure 5.1.

Figure 5.1
Strategy Types and Dimensions in Global Industries

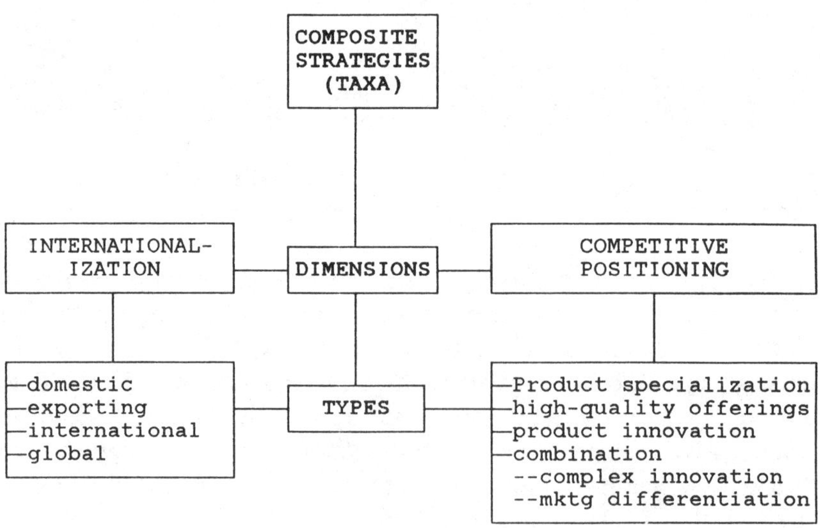

The partitioning of composite business strategies provides a conceptually consistent framework for discussing the types of internationalization and competitive positioning activities that characterize the four-group classification. Strategy types associated with each of these two dimensions of business strategy will be discussed in the next section, first separately and then in combination.

THE INTERNATIONALIZATION STRATEGY DIMENSION

Four broad types of internationalization strategy were identified in the businesses studied. These include: (1) "domestic," (2) "exporting," (3) "international," and (4) "global" strategy dimensions. These four internationalization strategy types were broadly interpreted from the emphasis that businesses placed on political, investment, and integration activities as they transcended national boundaries. Clear differences in how businesses stressed these conceptualized substrategies enabled the identification of a discriminating internationalization strategy dimension. Each of the four internationalization strategy types will now be discussed.

The Domestic Strategy

Understandably, the internationalization dimension played a very minor role in defining domestic strategies. Instead, overall strategic behavior was dominated by competitive positioning. Little emphasis was placed on international investment, political, or integration substrategies.

These findings are consistent with much of the strategy classification work conducted using solely domestic samples. As discussed in Chapter 2, studies using largely domestic samples have failed to find that variables associated with international aspects of competition discriminate overall business strategy. It is not surprising, then, that domestic strategies place little emphasis on international strategy dimensions.

The Exporting Strategy

When compared with strictly domestic businesses, exporting businesses relied much more heavily on international sales in accounting for total business revenues. Furthermore, businesses were commonly committed to increasing international sales levels through eventual foreign direct investment, typically in terms of overseas sales/distribution centers.

Exporting businesses placed considerable attention on international external integration and international political activities. Integration with the international external environment was achieved largely through developing expansive international information networks and establishing licensing agreements based principally on manufacturing technology. In terms of international political activities, particular attention was focused on lobbying foreign governments to ease import restrictions and pressuring the U.S. government or its agencies to assist the business in penetrating foreign markets.

The International Strategy

With increased levels of international activity, businesses became more fully exposed to divergent international business environments. This exposure had a dramatic influence on strategic behavior, as businesses found themselves stretched to balance global competitive pressures with organizational capabilities that remain dominated by domestic concerns.

This balance was best exemplified by Group 3 businesses that seemed to pursue "compromise" patterns of international strategic behavior. These patterns were characterized by (1) high levels of international investment and trade, (2) the presence of dominant U.S. operations, (3) the striving to efficiently transfer U.S.-developed products and production processes to overseas markets, and (4) the refining of product offerings to meet local market demands. Product refinements were typically carried out locally—often involving reexports of older-generation products to less sophisticated international markets.

The international literature that relates specifically to Group 3 businesses focuses primarily on the viability of either "multifocal" or "international" strategies. A *multifocal strategy*, as discussed by Prahalad and Doz, refers to the simultaneous pursuance of both global efficiencies and national responsiveness.[2] Given the trade-offs involved, a multifocal strategy is more of an intermediate strategy type that Prahalad and Doz suggest is appropriate "for smaller, weaker competitors in a number of industries in which governments themselves seek a tradeoff between control and competitiveness."[3] Bartlett and Ghoshal provide an extension to the multifocal classification by highlighting the importance that managing "the product life-cycle efficiently and flexibly plays in effectively balancing the concurrent demands for integration and responsiveness."[4] This strategy type is referred to by Bartlett and Ghoshal as an *international* strategy. Because of the importance that managing the product lifecycle played in Group 3 businesses, the strategy type associated by this group was identified as international.[5]

The international strategy type identified in this study was based on effectively exploiting domestically developed technologies by controlling how and when they are introduced to overseas markets. International investments were contingent on market opportunities for introducing the particular technology. Minimizing costs played a relatively minor role in determining the location of overseas operations. Also, rather than trying to influence their political environments proactively, international strategies seemed to be much more reactive. A high propensity existed either (1) to enter independently only those foreign markets that provided attractive political environments or (2) to avoid political entanglements entirely by seeking local partners to assist in product assembly and distribution.

The Global Strategy

Of the four internationalization strategy types identified, the "global" strategy type (Group 4 businesses) demonstrated the highest commitment to international activities. This commitment was directed by tight head office control over all international activities. International investment location decisions were determined on the basis of potential comparative advantage. Value activities were frequently spread across national boundaries leading to huge scale economies. Product design and development were either U.S based or the product of international research and development coalitions. Production-sharing alliances were used frequently. Worldwide distribution networks were established to move the business's internationally standardized products. Distribution often involved the sharing of outlets with sister businesses within the same corporate organization.

The global strategy type identified in this study differed along several important dimensions from those patterns commonly suggested in the literature. Conceptually, global business strategies have been portrayed as involving the leveraging of activities in one part of the world for the benefit of activities in a more strategically important location.[6] This systemic management of activities is the basis of a global strategy. One outcome of such a worldwide perspective is the business's low level of commitment to any particular national market.[7] Global strategies, by demanding a global perspective, work to reduce the influence of home nations on businesses. If the integrity of the system is to be maintained, the global business cannot, in principle, differentiate national markets by embracing some type of mixed multidomestic position.

Interestingly, this study found no clear evidence of the "homeless" global competitor described in the literature. Rather, the businesses in this study were all strongly committed to market position in the United States and were not prepared to sacrifice materially these positions for some form of hypothetical global advantage. Indeed, the U.S. market provided the majority of sales and served as the location of choice for product design, development, and manufacture. Also, while value activities were spread around the world, integration and market orientation were regional or continental; instead of perceiving the entire world as a competitive arena, continents or regions such as western Europe, South America, and the Pacific Rim served as competitive arenas.

Relating Internationalization Strategy Types

The businesses competing in global industries all emphasized different strategy types associated with the internationalization strategy dimension. At one extreme, businesses concentrated activities on domestic markets. At the other extreme, businesses took a more global perspective of their competitive environment. Somewhere in between these polar extremes businesses pursued broad international and exporting strategies. The relationship between domestic, exporting, international, and global strategy types is shown in Figure 5.2.

Figure 5.2
Continuum of Internationalization Strategy Types

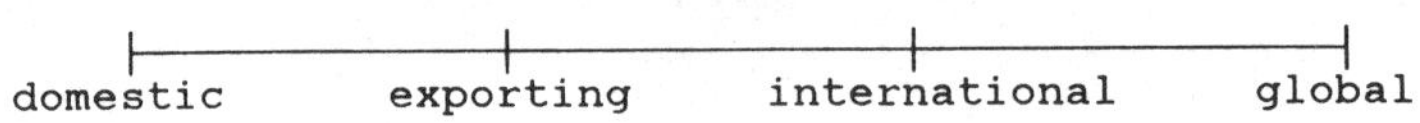

As shown in Figure 5.2, the exporting strategy type is positioned between the domestic and international strategy types because of its relatively low commitment to the internationalization strategy dimension. While the domestic strategy type demonstrates virtually no commitment to internationalization, the exporting, international, and global strategy types represent increasing levels of commitment to the internationalization strategy dimension.[8] In addition to variance associated with internationalization, significant differences in business group emphasis on competitive positioning are critical in determining overall composite strategies.

THE COMPETITIVE POSITIONING STRATEGY DIMENSION

As discussed in Chapter 2, much of the strategy classification research conducted in the 1970s and 1980s has been focused on differentiating businesses according to competitive positioning. This section is designed to provide a more complete discussion of competitive positioning strategy types while relating these types to patterns commonly emphasized in the strategic management literature. From this review it becomes evident that considerable commonality exists between business emphasis on competitive positioning strategy types, irrespective of broader industry contexts.

In this study four distinct competitive positioning strategy types were identified in businesses competing in global industries. These were (1) "product specialization," (2) "high-quality offerings," (3) "product innovation," and (4) "combination" based on complex innovation and marketing. Each of these four broad competitive positioning strategy types will now be discussed in more detail.

The Product Specialization Strategy

Businesses emphasizing a "domestic" internationalization strategy type also strongly supported competitive positioning based on producing specialty products. Product specialization is a dimension of what can be considered a differentiated focus strategy, where a business targets its products on a particular portion of a product line.[9] Whereas competitors offer a broad array of products both at home and abroad, businesses competing with a domestic product specialization strategy concentrated on narrow ranges of product offerings that are typically ignored by others. Production was centered on mature products in slow-growth market segments. Although marketing played a relatively minor role in achieving competitive advantage, products and services were designed to exploit the special needs of buyers that could not or were not being met by more broadly focused competitors.

By focusing production on only a few specialty products, important manufacturing skills and efficiencies were gained. Low cost was, however, regarded as an outcome of specialization rather than an end unto itself. In no instance were businesses found to be overall low-cost leaders in their respective industries. Also, the specialized nature of the products offered meant that cost rarely became an important competitive factor.

Competitive positioning strategies based on product specialization have been frequently suggested in the literature, again largely rooted in domestic samples. Since as far back as Barnard, authors have suggested that specialization provides the embodiment of organizational purpose.[10] Selznick, for example, asserted that specialization not only provides organizational purpose but determines the distinctive competence of the organization.[11] The product specialization strategy type also has considerable support in the strategy classification research. For example, Miles and Snow's "defender" strategy is characterized by a narrow product-market domain with primary attention focused on improving the efficiency of existing manufacturing operations.[12] In another example, C. Galbraith and Schendel identified "niche" strategies according to product specialization.[13] Also, both Roth and Davis identified competing on the basis of "specialty products" as a generic pattern of strategic behavior.[14]

In global industries, Porter has suggested that one way of achieving competitive advantage is through focusing competitive positioning on product specialization.[15] Support for the coupling of domestic strategic focus with specialization in global industries is provided by Cvar.[16] In her study of competition in global industries, Cvar identified three composite strategies, one of which was labeled "global focus." This pattern of strategic behavior was noted when

> the nationally-focused firm dominated a segment of the market with idiosyncratic demand, outside of the standardized product line of the global efficiency competitor and therefore uneconomical for the global participant to serve. These demands represented special product needs of the end-user.[17]

Again, these patterns generally coincided with the identification of the "domestic, product specialization" composite strategy in this study.

The High-Quality Offerings Strategy

Businesses emphasizing the "exporting" strategy type also stressed competitive positioning based on providing "high-quality offerings." High-quality offerings extended to the nature of both the products and the services offered to customers. Businesses emphasizing high-quality offerings tended to concentrate production on mature, high-quality products with product development activities centered on cosmetic changes that provided greater value to customers. Customer value was also increased through greater attention to product detail and quality of inputs. High-quality service included both in-house credit offerings and after-sales service. Special attention was placed on attracting and retaining long-term customers.

Considerable evidence is available in the strategic management literature to support a competitive positioning strategy type based on high-quality offerings. A variety of authors, including W. Hall, Abell, Porter, and Murray, have regarded competing on the basis of high-quality products and offerings as an important dimension of a differentiation strategy.[18] Within the domain of strategy classification research, Davis identified one particular group according to its emphasis on "customer service and product quality."[19] This group Davis labeled "antiquated traditionists." In a similar manner, Hambrick identified one of three high-profit clusters for disciplined capital goods makers by its emphasis on high-quality products and services.[20] Hambrick labeled this cluster "high-quality gendarme."[21]

The Product Innovation Strategy

Businesses competing with an "international strategy" strongly emphasized "product innovation" as a means of achieving competitive advantage. The importance of product innovation as a type of competitive positioning has been strongly supported in the literature.[22] Product innovation has also been specifically highlighted in the literature as a dominant competitive positioning strategy type in global industries.[23]

Competitive positioning based on product innovation involved a high emphasis on introducing major new products for international markets. Typically, however, product innovation work was carried out in the United States. This is consistent with Cvar who found that in businesses competing in global industries "the main R&D facility was located in the lead technological and volume markets,"[24] which in this case was the United States. Only in rare instances were ideas for innovative products generated by overseas competitors.

The process of offering highly innovative products typically involved a strong linkage between marketing and R&D personnel. Major new products were often suggested by marketing personnel and developed and revised by engineering personnel. According to Ohmae, this drive for market-driven innovation can provide

> a way to flourish without being forced to go head-to-head with competitors in either a low-cost or an upmarket game. Such a course exists—indeed, it leads managers back to the heart of what strategy is all about: creating value.[25]

Innovative, state-of-the-art products also tended to be high-priced products. These findings mirror those of Cvar who also found a strong correlation between product innovation and price in global industries.[26] Innovative products seem to demand premium pricing. Moving these "high-prestige," high-tech products requires an increased emphasis on skilled sales. Marketing is based on perpetuating the image of "state of the art" across a variety of product lines within the same industry.

The Combination Strategy

Businesses emphasizing the "global strategy" type of the internationalization strategy dimension also emphasized a combination competitive positioning strategy. This combination strategy type represented an interaction between both complex innovation and marketing differentiation. While both complex innovation and marketing differentiation could have potentially been observed as individual competitive positioning strategy types, a combination of the two was associated with the identification of a discrete, independent strategy type.

As separate competitive positioning strategy types, complex innovation and marketing differentiation have each been strongly emphasized in the literature. Complex innovation, according to Miller, "involves the degree to which the firm introduces major new products or services—not simple or cosmetic departures from previous offerings."[27] Porter suggests that complex innovation not only encompasses the role of formal R&D within the organization but "must also be broader because of the pervasive impact of technology on the value chain."[28] In addition to Porter and Miller, Miller and Friesen, Miles and Snow, and Hambrick have all suggested business strategy types that are similar to the complex innovation strategy identified in this study.[29] In a global industry context, the notion that global strategies are rooted in high levels of technological change also has considerable support.[30]

In discussing complex innovation, Porter argues that it should be designed to achieve either an overall low cost or differentiation strategy.[31] Global strategies based on complex innovation were focused primarily on product rather than process technology. Product technological change, while considerate of overall needs for production efficiency, was nevertheless largely intended to enhance product differentiation. Final products did not represent low-cost budget offerings. Rather, attention to quality, in terms of conforming to product specifications, was stressed.

Concurrent with the pursuance of complex innovation, businesses competing with global combination strategies also strongly emphasized marketing differentiation. Marketing differentiation represented a strong emphasis on marketing activities including marketing research, promotion, advertising, and control over channels of distribution. According to Miller, marketing differentiation "strives to create customer loyalty by uniquely meeting a particular need."[32] In this case, marketing differentiation was focused on building industry reputation for technology, quality, reliability, and permanence in given host markets.

Various studies have shown that, irrespective of industry context, marketing differentiation can play a vital role in determining competitive advantage. In addition to Miller, Porter identified marketing as fundamental in a successful differentiation strategy.[33] In another example, Davis, in his classification of business strategies from a largely domestic sample, identified a generic "promoters" strategy as an autonomous pattern of strategic behavior. This strategy was characterized by a strong emphasis on both marketing and distribution factors.[34] Others who have stressed the importance marketing differentiation plays in determining competitive positioning include Ghemawat, who included marketing differentiation as one of three means of achieving competitive advantage, and Kotler, who refers to the pursuance of competitive advantage through differentiation as "megamarketing."[35]

With regard to the efficiency of pursuing both cost and differentiation strategies, Porter has suggested that businesses emphasizing a combination of competitive positioning strategy types are "almost guaranteed low profitability."[36] To Porter "only the three generic strategies are alternative, viable approaches to dealing with the competitive forces."[37] However, as has been discussed in Chapter 2, the exclusivity of Porter's cost, differentiation, and focus strategies has been only partially empirically supported by Dess and Davis, White, and Woo and Cool.[38]

These same researchers have also suggested that some combinations of these strategy taxa (cost, differentiation, focus) often result in superior performance. Here, the central issue is focused on the proper level of abstraction in conceptualizing generic strategies. As such, cost, differentiation, and focus (or their derivatives) have been equally viewed as representative of lower levels of abstraction and as such are more appropriately considered as strategy "types" or "strategic factors" that *in combination make up the taxa* or composite strategies.[39]

A combination of conceptual and empirical evidence is offered to support this contention. Conceptually, Murray argues that "combining both the product differentiation and cost leadership strategies should be feasible in many industries" and that just as generic strategies outperform less defined strategies, "by combining both [of Porter's] generic strategies successfully, a firm should be able to outcompete rivals that pursue only one strategy."[40] In a similar manner, Hill argues against the exclusivity of Porter's strategies, citing two main problems:

> First, differentiation can be a means for firms to achieve an overall low-cost position [through increasing volume, which leads to learning effects, economies of scale, and economies of scope]. Second, there are many situations in which establishing a sustained competitive advantage requires the firm to simultaneously pursue both low-cost and differentiation strategies because in many industries there is no unique low-cost position.[41]

In this context, the actual generic strategy pursued by a business is represented by emphasis placed on combinations of competitive positioning strategy types.

Empirical evidence also seems to support these arguments. Supporting the contention that combination strategies may more accurately reflect generic strategies is Davis, who identified ten generic groups; Robinson and Pearce, who suggest five strategic groups; and C. Galbraith and Schendel, who developed six strategic groups for consumer goods businesses and four strategic groups for industrial products businesses.[42] In each of these cases, strategic factors or characteristics were identified at lower levels of abstraction that were consistent with those suggested by Porter, Dess and Davis, White, Woo and Cool, and Miller.[43] Again, it becomes a matter of perspective, or level of analysis.

Relating Competitive Positioning Strategy Types

Of the four broad competitive positioning types identified, three were found to represent variations of differentiation strategies (product specialization, high-quality offerings, and product innovation), and one was found to represent a combination strategy. In contrast to the conceptual and case evidence suggested by Davidson and Haspeslagh, Hout, Porter, and Rudden, Cvar, Hamel and Prahalad, Porter, and Jolly, *there was no empirical support of a dominant low-cost strategy type* in the businesses competing in the global industries studied.[44] This finding is consistent with the research of both Murray and Hill, who address the relationship between cost and differentiation strategies in a broad contingency perspective of competition.[45] Additional support is also provided by Ohmae, and Doz and Prahalad.[46]

A major argument that both Murray and Hill develop is that cost leadership is not a viable strategy option in many industries.[47] This reasoning is rooted in two related concepts: (1) "the exogenous preconditions for a viable cost leadership strategy stem principally from the industry's structural characteristics," and (2) within that industry "a cost leadership strategy is viable only if cost structures vary across competitors . . . in ways other than in direct ratio to output."[48] According to Hill, this suggests that in order to become the low-cost competitor in an industry "there is a unique cost leadership position that can be occupied by only one firm at any given time."[49] Simply put, in many industries structural limitations may make an overall low-cost strategy untenable.

Both Ohmae, and Doz and Prahalad have discussed the difficulty of pursuing a low-cost strategy to a global industry contingency.[50] Ohmae argues that competitive advantage is rarely achieved by shifting production to low labor cost countries in the global configuration of value activities. Three reasons are cited: (1) cheap labor also tends to be poorly trained labor with lower levels of productivity; (2) the importance of labor costs in the delivered cost of products is shrinking with technological changes; and (3) as workers become better trained in low-income countries, expectations and wages rise rapidly. In a similar manner, Doz and Prahalad assert that global competitors are converging in cost levels not only with regard to labor but across a broad array of factors:

> Parallel arguments can be made about other competitive parameters such as capital costs and economies of scale. While they still all differ from global competitor to global competitor, they seldom provide a strong enough basis for successful competitive attacks.[51]

From a purely industry context, conceptual evidence seems to support this study's findings that competition in global industries need not be based solely on low cost. Consequently, given the organizational and international contextual constraints that characterize global competition, it should not seem particularly surprising that low cost was not found to typify competition in global industries.

COMPOSITE STRATEGIES IN GLOBAL INDUSTRIES

Two separate dimensions of business strategy in global industries have been discussed: competitive positioning, relating to the nature of competition within a given market environment, and internationalization, relating to how and where the business positions its activities in actually accessing a particular market. In the broadest of senses, internationalization strategy types govern how the business tangibly comes into contact with the customer through the international coordination and configuration of value activities, whereas competitive positioning determines how the business actually appeals to customers' needs, once it has a capability of delivering a good or service. Competitive positioning and internationalization, while separate dimensions of business strategy, are not mutually exclusive. Rather, they are two essential components that every business *must* specify in developing an overall strategy. Indeed, both dimensions work synergistically to determine overall patterns of strategic behavior or, in the development of a strategy classification, actual composite strategies.

As components of these two broad dimensions, eight distinct strategy types have been identified. In the case of the internationalization dimension, these strategy types include domestic, exporting, international, and global strategy characteristics. These strategy types as identified are not mutually exclusive. This is illustrated by businesses emphasizing the global strategy type; these same businesses were also observed heavily supporting both domestic activities and the exporting of finished goods. Rather, every business more strongly emphasizes one of the four internationalization strategy types. In a similar manner, four competitive positioning strategy types have been identified and include product specialization, high-quality offerings, product innovation, and a combination of complex innovation and marketing differentiation. These dimensional strategy types, too, are not mutually exclusive, as is illustrated in the case of combination strategies. Again, one of the competitive positioning strategy types is more strongly emphasized than the others.

Beyond identifying the broad strategy types themselves, interrelationships between internationalization and competitive positioning have been identified. These interrelationships represent the establishment of possible composite strategies that serve as the foundation for the classification. Using a 4×4 matrix of strategy types, a possible combination of 16 composite strategies emerges. However, the design of this classification is based on capturing the dominant patterns that link certain strategy types. Using this approach, four principal composite strategies have been identified for businesses competing in global industries: (1) "domestic, product specialization," (2) "exporting, high-quality offerings," (3) "international, product innovation," and (4) "global, combination" based on complex innovation and marketing differentiation.

Composite Strategies and the International Literature

Similar attempts to capture the "main threads" of business strategy in broad international environments have been made in the literature. Fayerweather, for example, suggests four composite strategies or types that show remarkable similarity to the four taxa identified here.[52] These four strategies are identified as the (1) dynamic high technology model, (2) stable or low technology model, (3) advanced management skill model, and (4) unified logistic, labor transmission model. In that Fayerweather portrays these as generic strategies, any of these four could potentially be represented in global industries.

Fayerweather's "dynamic high technology" strategy strongly resembles the "international, product innovation" strategy identified in this study. This strategy is based on the centralization of R&D, the continual flow of innovative products and processes, and the tight control over international high-technology transfers. Similarly, certain aspects of Fayerweather's "stable, low technology" strategy are closely related to the "exporting, high-quality offerings" strategy identified in this study. In both the "stable, low technology" and "exporting, high-quality offerings" strategies, products represent standardized technology whose export brings fast financial returns. Overall levels of international involvement are low, as is the business's bargaining power in the host nation. Fayerweather's "unified logistics, labor transmission" strategy is also very similar to the "global, combination" strategy identified in this study. Products have high value-to-weight ratios, production is shifted to low labor cost countries, and competition is premised on the effective marketing of globally standardized products. "Global, combination" strategies would also borrow heavily from Fayerweather's "advanced managerial skill" model in that, according to Doz and Prahalad, global competitors will increasingly rely on management quality as a source of competitive advantage.[53] However, other aspects of Fayerweather's "advanced managerial skill" model would be more applicable to "multifocal" strategies—which were not identified in this study—than to "global, combination" strategies. Finally, given that Fayerweather's objective was to develop a classification of international strategies, it is not surprising that there is no accounting of the "domestic, product specialization" strategies also identified in global industries.

Although several similarities link Fayerweather's four broad patterns of international strategy with the four identified composite strategies in global industries, Fayerweather's classification has several shortcomings that should not be overlooked. One problem is that he is not specific as to how he developed the classification scheme or on what theoretical foundations it is built. A second problem is that Fayerweather fails to distinguish effectively between corporate- and business-level strategies. While his classification is expressly focused on "MNC strategy," the patterns he identifies are not consistent with corporate-level strategy.

The level-of-analysis problem extends to the classification itself where Fayerweather suggests that indeed "the strategies of many firms combine the characteristics of two or more [strategy models]."[54] Here, Fayerweather seems to be suggesting that in many cases the composite strategies of businesses are not captured by his four strategy models. Rather, these models alternatively represent either strategy components or final composite strategies. The potential interactive effect of combining "two or more" models or characteristics of models is not explored. The result is confusion over the appropriate unit of analysis and failure of the classification to group parsimoniously businesses according to distinct patterns of emphasis.

Another major problem with Fayerweather's classification is that each of his four strategy types could just as easily describe a domestic competitor as an international competitor. The international "twist" that Fayerweather does include in describing each strategy type is regarded as secondary in importance to the technology base or skill levels of the MNCs in question. Such technology assets could just as easily be deployed in a strictly domestic context as in a more international one. The result is an international strategy classification scheme with very little specificity about actual patterns of international configuration. Fayerweather's classification, while ambitious in its attempts to capture common patterns in international business strategy, is expressly weak in its ability to differentiate discrete patterns of strategic behavior as businesses compete internationally.

Another popularized classification of business strategies is Porter's generic strategies (cost, differentiation, or focus).[55] As previously discussed, these generic strategies can be related directly to the competitive positioning strategy types identified in this study. Product specialization, high-quality offerings, and product innovation are all derivatives of Porter's differentiation strategy; the combination strategy type identified in this study relates to Porter's cost and differentiation strategies.

As discussed in Chapter 2, Porter also suggests four strategic alternatives in global industries: broad line global competition, global focus, national focus, and protected niche. These broad patterns resemble aspects of the internationalization dimension identified in this study. For example, the domestic strategy type identified in this study is closely related to Porter's national focus strategy. However, the regionally focused global competitor identified in this study is not accounted for by Porter in his classification. Porter also does not mention either exporting or mixed international strategy types.

Porter has yet to distinguish fully his conceptualization of global strategy in terms of internationalization and competitive positioning. Indeed, his own perspectives of global strategy seem to have matured with time, perhaps as a result of mounting criticism leveled against his cost/differentiation generic strategies. To Porter, the essence of a global strategy can be captured through strategic focus.[56] Yet by defining global industries through international parameters, it becomes imperative to determine both whether and how member businesses are actually competing internationally. Later Porter expands his earlier conceptualization of global strategy by defining it as "one in which a firm seeks to gain competitive advantage from its international presence through either concentrating configuration, coordination among dispersed activities, or both."[57] With this definition, global strategy is no longer portrayed as simply a function of the unidimensional geographic exposure captured by strategic focus. Rather, it is reflected in the essence of internationalization captured in this study.

Porter has always faced a difficult challenge subordinating his own four—largely internationalization—strategy types to his dominant generic strategies. Indeed, by identifying global strategies through predominantly internationalization, Porter is seen implicitly supporting a *concurrent* strategic emphasis on both competitive positioning and internationalization. For example, a broad-line global competitor will compete either on the basis of low cost or differentiation. Thus, cost and differentiation are dimensions of a global strategy, and likewise a global strategy is rooted in cost or differentiation advantages.

Mapping Business Strategies in Global Industries

Many of the shortcomings with both Fayerweather's and Porter's attempts to develop a classification of international business strategy rest with their failure to distinguish adequately the difference between how the business positions its activities across national borders and how the business appeals to particular customer needs. An appreciation of this two-dimensional perspective of international competition has become more common among researchers who have begun to focus on the relationship between the pressures for global integration and the pressures for local responsiveness.[58] Response to this "dual imperative" determines business internationalization and competitive positioning within a given host environment.

Perhaps the best developed discussion of the dual imperative is provided by Prahalad and Doz, who suggest the "integration-responsiveness" (IR) grid to provide "a way of capturing the pressures on a given business" in an international context.[59] The IR grid is shown in Figure 5.3.The vertical

Figure 5.3
Integration-Responsiveness Grid: Strategic Focus and Organizational Adaptation

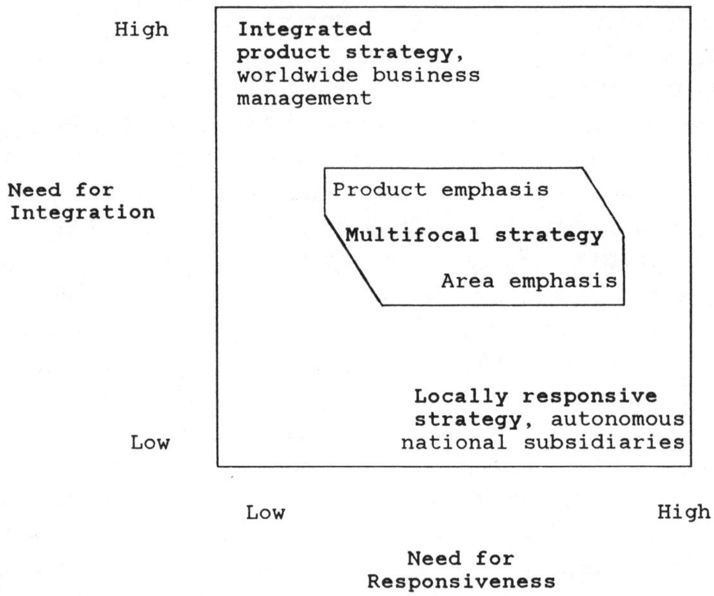

Adapted from: Prahalad and Doz (1987: 25).

axis in Figure 5.3—"Need for Integration"—reflects industry constraints affecting the competitive positioning of businesses. In contrast, the horizontal axis—"Need for Responsiveness"—represents industry demand parameters that potentially transcend host nations. According to Prahalad and Doz, appropriate business strategies, given these environmental imperatives, vary from the global integration strategy in the upper-left-hand corner, through the multifocal strategy in the center of the figure, to the local responsiveness strategy in the bottom-right-hand corner of the figure.[60] Even within the context of a global industry, it has been posited that these three strategy types will be evident.[61] This would be demonstrated as businesses partition global industries into key segments.

By better understanding the environmental pressures of the dual imperative and by integrating the work of Prahalad and Doz, and Porter, the IR grid provides a useful framework from which to map this study's identified business strategies in global industries. Using Porter's framework, the vertical axis would represent business competitive positioning responses to industry pressures, resulting in either a low-cost strategy at one extreme or differentiation at the other.[62] As such, Prahalad and Doz's "locally responsive strategy" would result in competitive positioning being overwhelmingly based on product differentiation according to local market demand.[63] Similarly, Prahalad and Doz's "integrated product strategy" would result in the competitive positioning strategy dimension being overwhelmingly based on reducing costs through internationalization.[64] Internationalization strategy types appropriate for these contextual pressures ranging from global to domestic integration have been shown in Figure 5.2 and can be seen varying according to the external need for responsiveness. Together, both the vertical and horizontal axes, which in Figure 5.3 represent to Prahalad and Doz both endogenous and exogenous pressures, can be related to dimensions of strategic behavior consistent with the work of Porter as well as those authors contributing to the development of Figure 5.2. The positioning of the four groups of businesses following distinct composite strategies identified in this study are shown in Figure 5.4.

In Figure 5.4, each of the four groups is shown to emphasize discrete patterns of strategic behavior. All four groups are represented along the horizontal axis by emphasis placed on internationalization strategy types. These range from domestic to global.[65]

Along the vertical axis, all four groups are represented by their emphasis on competitive positioning strategy types. As illustrative of the broad competitive positioning strategy dimension, the vertical axis to Porter would represent a trade-off between low cost and differentiation. At the upper extreme, for example, competitive positioning would be dominated by an emphasis on strategy types directly related to low cost; at the lower extreme, competitive positioning would be dominated by derivatives of Porter's differentiation strategy. Business emphasizing neither extreme would base overall competitive positioning on strategy types representing varying levels of support for both low cost and differentiation.

Figure 5.4
Mapping Strategy Groups: Relating Porter's Generic Strategies to the IR Grid

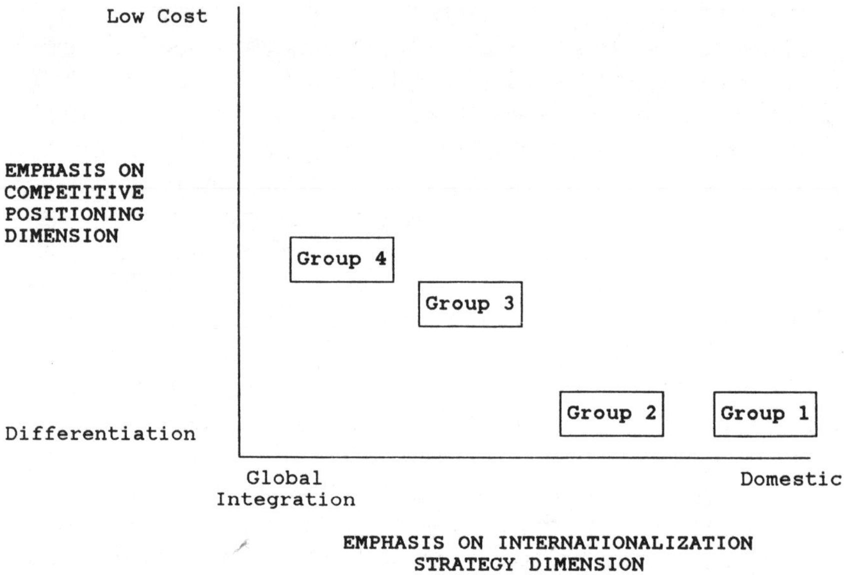

<u>NOTE</u>: **Group** 1--Domestic, Product Specialization

Group 2--Exporting, High-Quality Offering

Group 3--International, Product Innovation

Group 4--Global, Combination
--Complex Innovation
--Marketing Differentiation

In this study, Groups 1 and 2 ("product specialization," and "high-quality offerings") were found to stress strongly competitive positioning strategy types directly related to Porter's differentiation strategy. Low cost did not play a significant role in determining competitive positioning. In contrast, in Groups 3 and 4 ("product innovation" and "combination," respectively) aspects of low cost did play a role in determining overall competitive positioning. This was most pronounced for Group 4 businesses where complex innovation often resulted in cost advantages. Here, however, low cost was found to be *one of several motivating factors* behind internationally configuring value activities. Low cost played an even less important role in the competitive positioning of Group 3 businesses. These businesses were also constrained to compete on the basis of costs, yet this was for only a small portion of their product lines in certain geographic markets. Clearly, with both Groups 3 and 4, differentiation-related strategy types still represented the bulk of the overall competitive positioning strategy dimension.

SUMMARY

This chapter has provided a more thorough examination of the four composite strategies identified in global industries. In particular, the strategy types that comprise the internationalization and competitive positioning dimensions of composite strategies were discussed, first individually and then in combination. It was observed that both dimensions play a critical role in determining strategy content in global industries. Furthermore, a two-dimensional framework for identifying strategy content facilitated the mapping of strategies according to business emphasis of the different dimensions. Here, it was observed that the global low-cost and multifocal strategy types posited in the literature were not evident in the businesses studied.

These findings raise several interesting questions about the role of business strategy/industry fit. What is the relationship between composite strategies and the industry pressures that determine the critical global contingency? What are the performance implications of pursuing different composite strategies? And finally, does industry-strategy fit influence performance? Chapter 6 is designed to respond to these important questions.

NOTES

1. Prahalad and Doz (1987).
2. Ibid.
3. Ibid., p. 97.
4. See Bartlett and Ghoshal (1987a: 10). Beyond the failure to recognize the need for organizational learning, multifocal strategies also have the disadvantage of suggesting a type of "stuck in the middle" internationalization strategy type. Porter earlier addressed the difficulty of being stuck in the middle by concurrently pursuing cost and differentiation competitive positioning strategy types. Bartlett and Ghoshal's addition to organization learning and the international management of the product life cycle add unique proactive elements to the internationalization strategy type.
5. An "international" strategy type as described by Bartlett and Ghoshal is also identified by high levels of local market feedback accompanied by a commitment to organizational learning. The subtle distinction between Bartlett and Ghoshal's international strategy type and the Group 3 strategy type is recognized but not deemed as fundamental in relabeling the classification.

6. See Hout, Porter, and Rudden (1982), Porter (1986a), Prahalad and Doz (1987), Jolly (1988), and Ghoshal (1987).

7. Vernon (1979) and Doz (1986).

8. Typically, international strategy continuums of this form extend from multi-domestic to global. See, for example, Bartlett (1985) and Porter (1986a). However, a multidomestic strategy type—involving autonomous subsidiaries that adopt corporate offerings from a variety of business units—is most clearly associated with a corporate-level construct and is thus inconsistent with the unit of analysis utilized in this study.

9. Porter (1985).

10. Barnard (1938).

11. Selznick (1957).

12. Miles and Snow (1978).

13. C. Galbraith and Schendel (1983).

14. Roth (1986) and Davis (1986).

15. Porter (1980).

16. Cvar (1984).

17. Ibid., p. 316.

18. Abell (1980), Porter (1980), W. Hall (1980), and Murray (1988).

19. Davis (1986).

20. Hambrick (1983b).

21. Ibid.

22. See, for example, Ghemawat (1986), Hambrick (1983b), Miles and Snow (1978), Miller (1987b, 1988), Mintzberg (1979b), Porter (1980), and Takeuchi and Nonaka (1986).

23. See, for example, Cvar (1984), Hamel and Prahalad (1985), Ohmae (1985), Jolly (1988), and Ghoshal (1987).

24. Cvar (1984: 298).

25. Ohmae (1988: 151).

26. Cvar (1984).

27. Miller (1987b: 57).

28. Porter (1985: 176).

29. Miller and Friesen (1978), Miles and Snow (1978), and Hambrick (1983b).

30. See, for example, Hout, Porter, and Rudden (1982), Cvar (1984), Ohmae (1985), Porter (1986b), Flaherty (1986), and Doz (1987).

31. Porter (1985: 177).

32. Miller (1987b: 57).

33. See Porter (1980) and Miller (1986, 1987b).

34. Davis (1986).

35. Ghemawat (1986) and Kotler (1986).

36. Porter (1980: 41).

37. Ibid., p. 41.

38. Porter (1980), Dess and Davis (1984), White (1986), and Woo and Cool (1983).

39. A caveat to this perspective of generic strategies as combination strategies is the somewhat equivocal assertion by Dess and Davis (1984) that, irrespective of the level of abstraction, strategic factors mirror the generic strategies of businesses.

40. Murray (1988: 396).

41. Hill (1988: 401).

42. See Davis (1986), Robinson and Pearce (1985), and C. Galbraith and Schendel (1983).

43. See Porter (1980), Dess and Davis (1984), White (1986), Woo and Cool (1983), and Miller (1987a).

44. See Davidson and Haspeslagh (1982), Hout, Porter, and Rudden (1982), Cvar (1984), Hamel and Prahalad (1985), Porter (1986a), and Jolly (1988).

45. Murray (1988) and Hill (1988).

46. See Ohmae (1985) and Doz and Prahalad (1988).

47. Murray (1988) and Hill (1988).

48. Murray (1988: 395, 392).

49. Hill (1988: 409).

50. Ohmae (1985) and Doz and Prahalad (1988).

51. Doz and Prahalad (1988: 347).

52. Fayerweather (1982).

53. Doz and Prahalad (1988).

54. Fayerweather (1982: 434).

55. Porter (1980).

56. Ibid.

57. Porter (1986a: 20).

58. Doz (1980), Bartlett (1985), Roth (1986), C. Galbraith and Kay (1986), and Prahalad and Doz (1987).

59. Prahalad and Doz (1987: 18).

60. Multifocal strategies represent reactions to industry pressures for both global integration and host nation responsiveness.

61. See Prahalad and Doz (1987) and Ghoshal (1987).

62. The elements of Porter's (1980) focus strategy that deal with nongeographic product segmentation would also be represented by the vertical axis (that is, low-cost focus, differentiation focus).

63. This contention that locally responsive strategies are rooted in typically inefficient product differentiation is strongly supported in the literature (Robinson, 1961; Keegan, 1969; Doz, 1980; White and Poynter, 1984; Herbert, 1984; and Bartlett and Ghoshal, 1987b).

64. Globally integrated product strategies are most frequently based on objectives of minimizing overall product costs. For example, Doz (1980) argues that a global integration is most appropriately designed to meet the economic imperative of overall cost efficiency. Furthermore, global strategies are by their very nature based on global products (Levitt, 1983) that are by design undifferentiated from one market to the next.

65. One important caveat is offered with regard to the positioning of Group 4's internationalization strategy along the horizontal axis. The extent of international market share battles suggested in the literature as demonstrative of global strategies was not found in Group 4 businesses. Rather, Group 4 businesses were more focused on regional market share battles. Also, from Figure 4.7, evidence suggests that the ratio of mean levels of international sales to total sales may be higher for businesses emphasizing an "international, product innovation" strategy than for businesses emphasizing a "global, combination" strategy. Taken together, the implication is that the global strategy type identified in this study should be positioned on the horizontal axis in Figure 5.4 to the right of the "quintessential" global strategy suggested in the literature.

CHAPTER 6

RELATING COMPOSITE STRATEGIES TO THE GLOBAL INDUSTRY CONTEXT

This chapter is designed to extend the discussion of the strategy classification by examining the performance implications of pursuing a particular composite strategy and by providing a more complete examination of the relationship between composite strategies and global industry imperatives. The chapter is organized into three main sections. The first section addresses the relationship between perceptual versus actual environments. Ten variables are identified that act as triggers to industry globalization, and perceptions of environmental imperatives are reported for each of the four strategic groups. The second section of the chapter maps out the industry perceptions of the four strategic groups and relates these perceptions to composite strategies. The final section of the chapter discusses the performance implications of poor fit between composite strategies and the perceived industry imperatives of the four strategic groups. Alternative causes for performance differentials are also explored.

RELATING COMPOSITE STRATEGIES TO INDUSTRY IMPERATIVES

Implicit in the identification of particular patterns of strategic behavior in global industries is the premise that performance outcomes are determined by effectively matching strategic behavior to critical environmental contingencies. Indeed, from a strategic management perspective, contingency theory holds that performance is a function of strategic responses to the organization's external context.[1] Furthermore, industry organization theory suggests that the industry context—extended in this case to the global industry—is the most critical contingency affecting the business unit. Given these theoretical underpinnings, performance measures can be used to ascertain the result of the goodness of fit between a given pattern of strategic behavior and a global industry environment.[2]

As presented in the Prahalad and Doz IR framework, businesses represented by global integration, multifocal, and locally responsive strategies can have equally effective levels of industry/strategy fit within their respective global industry contexts.[3] In the four groups identified in this study, the implication is that *if a proper match is achieved* between strategic behavior and industry imperatives, "international, product innovation," "exporting, high-quality offerings," "global, combination," and "domestic, product specialization" strategies should, on average, have equal performance levels.

The broader argument that performance is contingent on proper fit between strategy and industry structure is based on propositions forwarded by Prescott, Prahalad and Doz, Murray, and C. Hill.[4] Both Murray and Hill, in building on the work of Porter, attempt to develop a contingency perspective of generic strategies. Not only is any generic strategy potentially effective, but these authors argue that contingency linkages establish critical relationships between generic strategies and "external preconditions." Within the IR framework, Prahalad and Doz argue that strategic groups in global industries have differing *perceptions* of the pressures or imperatives for responsiveness and integration and consequently design strategies appropriate for these perceived contexts. In other words, although the industry may be global, businesses may perceive it to be something entirely different.[5] This problem of misidentifying industry pressures may be more acute in global industries than other generic industry contexts, given the high levels of environmental complexity and variance.[6]

In order to ascertain both the relative strengths of the industry pressures facing each group and the nature of the matches between perceptions of industry pressures and patterns of strategic behavior, a set of ten industry variables was identified. These variables represent an attempt to identify, within a global industry context, the extent of pressures for responsiveness and integration facing each strategic group. Here, McGee and Thomas suggest that

> adding the perceptual data drawn from individual decision-makers to the economic models of competition provided by industrial organization economics perspectives should enable a more general framework to be developed for identifying important [strategy contingency] variables.[7]

The specification of industry variables indicative of underlying structural environmental "triggers" that lead to changes in the globalization of industries has been suggested by a number of researchers.[8] This stream of research suggests that, within a global industry, specific buyer-related structural forces include (1) standardized consumer demands worldwide, (2) minimal or standardized local customer service requirements, (3) global awareness of products among buyer groups, (4) a concentrated international distribution infrastructure, and standardized product technology. Furthermore, suppliers exert industry pressures through their expectations of (6) standardized purchasing practices throughout the world. Pressures for local responsiveness and global integration are further influenced by (7) the presence of world-scale production economies, (8) government restraint of international tangible and intangible asset flows, (9) large international variances in factor costs, and the importance of (10) transportation costs in determining the final delivered price of the product.

Using these ten structural triggers, each of the four strategy groups' perceptions of the environment was examined. Industry variable means across the four identified groups are presented in Figure 6.1.

As is evident from Figure 6.1, perceptions of industry pressures were generally homogeneous across the four strategic groups. Interestingly, there were no individual groups that could be associated exclusively with either strongly global or strongly domestic integration/responsiveness pressures within the global industries studied. Also, perceptions of industry pressures were rarely unidimensional. Rather, groups tended to perceive industry pressures as mixtures of both integration and responsiveness pressures.

Of the ten industry variables, four significant differences were found between the groups. Because of the general homogeneity of the strategy groups, these four variables appear to be more important in determining the contextual variance of global industries, whereas the other variables are all descriptive of a global industry. These variables include measures of the worldwide standardization of buyer/customer needs, the susceptibility of value activities to scale economies, the extent of government

Figure 6.1
Industry Variable Means and Strategic Groups

INDUSTRY VARIABLE	GROUP 1	GROUP 2	GROUP 3	GROUP 4	FVALUE*
Buyer needs standardized	3.454	2.579	2.651	2.487	2.17*
Standardized purchasing	2.454	1.789	2.186	1.948	1.45
Concent'd dist. channels	2.545	2.789	2.690	3.237	1.83
Scale economies	3.400	3.158	3.476	4.105	4.78**
Product info. worldwide	3.545	3.474	3.791	3.947	1.09
Government restrainment	3.818	3.632	3.186	3.769	2.67*
Standardized technology	3.545	2.556	3.302	2.897	2.82**
Transportation costs	3.091	2.316	2.326	2.667	1.34
Local customer service	3.545	3.895	4.047	4.026	0.84
Factor costs vary	3.818	3.778	3.581	4.079	1.77

NOTE: Scale is 1 to 5, where

1 represents variable that is "not at all characteristic" of industry pressures;
5 represents variable that is "extremely characteristic" of industry pressures

Group 1--Domestic, Product Specialization

Group 2--Exporting, High-Quality Offerings

Group 3--International, Product Innovation

Group 4--Global, Combination--Complex Innovation
--Marketing Differentiation

* Significance of difference, $p > 0.10$
** Significance of difference, $p > 0.05$

restraint of international activities, and the worldwide standardization of technology.

While the strong emphasis that some groups placed on these variables was expected, some surprises were evident. For example, the notions (1) that buyer/customer needs are standardized worldwide and (2) that product technology is standardized worldwide have been central themes in the definition of global industries.[9] Surprisingly, however, the "global, combination" strategy group had the lowest perceptions of both these variables, whereas the "domestic, product specialization" group had the highest perceptions of the salience of these dimensions. Similarly, while it was expected (and confirmed) that the domestic group would perceive high levels of government control over international activities, it was not anticipated that the global strategy group would also perceive the same levels of restriction. However, the businesses in the global group, as expected, had the highest perceptions of pressures for global-scale economies of the four groups.

MAPPING CRITICAL PERCEPTIONS OF INDUSTRY IMPERATIVES

In observing perceptions of industry pressures for responsiveness and integration, both within groups and across groups, several broad patterns become evident. Just as patterns of strategic behavior were presented using the IR grid, perceptions of industry pressures can also be mapped using the framework developed by Prahalad and Doz.[10] Consequently, to assist in identifying patterns of environmental pressures better, Figure 6.2 is designed to map the perceptions of industry pressures using the IR grid. Figure 6.2 was developed using the industry variable means for each strategy group identified in Figure 6.1. While recognizing that among all four groups inconsistencies were evident in perceptions of the salience of industry pressures, the IR grid is a framework designed to accommodate the dichotomous pressures facing the groups.

As indicated in Figure 6.2, none of the strategy groups perceived their global industry context as representative of uniquely global pressures. Groups 3 and 4, while differing in the perceptual details of their industry contexts, appeared to share similar overall views of the pressures for integration and responsiveness that they confront. For example, Groups 3 and 4 both perceived higher pressures for concentrated worldwide distribution channels, global-scale economies, and worldwide product information than either Groups 1 or 2. Groups 3 and 4 also minimized the importance placed on transportation costs in determining the final cost of the product. These are all critical dimensions that represent pressures for global integration and lack of pressures for responsiveness. However, the strength of these industry pressures was also not extreme. In that these perceptions were generally consistent across groups but were sometimes inconsistent within each of the two groups, Groups 3 and 4 are presented in Figure 6.2 as sharing the same enlarged perceptions of industry pressures. These pressures together represented incentives for generally low levels of responsiveness and moderately high levels of global integration.

Figure 6.2
Mapping Critical Perceptions of the Industry Using the IR Grid

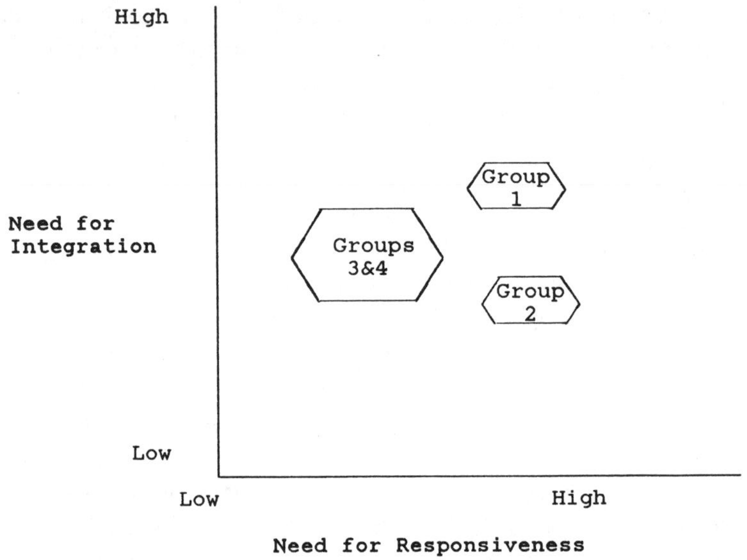

Group 1--Domestic, Product Specialization

Group 2--Exporting, High-Quality Offerings

Group 3--International, Product Innovation

Group 4--Global, Combination
--Complex Innovation
--Marketing Differentiation

In contrast, Group 1 businesses perceived higher overall levels of local responsiveness and similar levels of global integration pressures to businesses in Groups 3 and 4. This is seen by the high perceived industry pressures of worldwide standardized buyer needs, standardized purchasing practices, and standardized technology. This is contrasted by low perceived industry levels of concentrated worldwide distribution channels, worldwide product information, and high pressures for local responsiveness resulting from high transportation cost ratios. Again, levels were not extreme.

Group 2 was the most consistent in perceiving industry pressures. Overall, Group 2 perceived lower levels of integration pressures and higher levels of responsiveness pressures than Group 1. This is seen in low group means for international-scale economies, worldwide product information, worldwide standardized technology, and worldwide standardized purchasing. Other variables, while not at extreme levels, also indicated clear pressures for local responsiveness while deemphasizing pressures for global integration.

Industry Pressures and Composite Strategies

In reviewing Figures 5.4 and 6.2 it appears that in certain cases the match between broad patterns of strategic behavior and perceptions of industry pressures was not realized. These mismatches are shown in Figure 6.3, which represents the overlay of Figure 5.4 on Figure 6.2. In Figure 6.3, the vertical axis represents the competitive positioning dimension for mapping the composite strategies as well as the pressures for integration in mapping industry pressures as perceived by each of the respective strategic groups. Similarly, the horizontal axis in Figure 6.3 represents the internationalization dimension for mapping the composite strategies in addition to the pressures for local responsiveness.

Mismatches between composite strategies and perceptions of industry pressures are particularly pronounced in the case of Group 1, and to a lesser extent Group 2, businesses. Generally, tight matches were achieved between perceptions of industry pressures and patterns of strategic behavior with businesses in Groups 3 and 4.

Using the integration-responsiveness framework, Group 1 largely perceived industry pressures as multifocal, or dominated by simultaneous pressures to integrate activities globally and remain locally responsive. Yet in terms of strategic behavior, Group 1 businesses were strictly domestically focused, with no global integration. Thus, perceptions of industry pressures were not well matched with strategic behavior.

Similarly, Group 2 businesses demonstrated patterns of strategic behavior that were uncharacteristic of its perceptions of industry pressures. Perceptions of these pressures included moderately low needs for global integration combined with moderately high needs for local responsiveness. Yet in patterns of strategic behavior, Group 2 businesses placed far less emphasis on low cost than expected by perceptions of industry pressures. Emphasis on high-quality offerings was generally consistent with perceptions of pressures for local responsiveness.

In contrast to what appear to be mismatches between perceptions of environmental pressures and patterns of strategic behavior demonstrated

Figure 6.3
Mapping Strategy Groups and Perceptions of Industry Imperatives

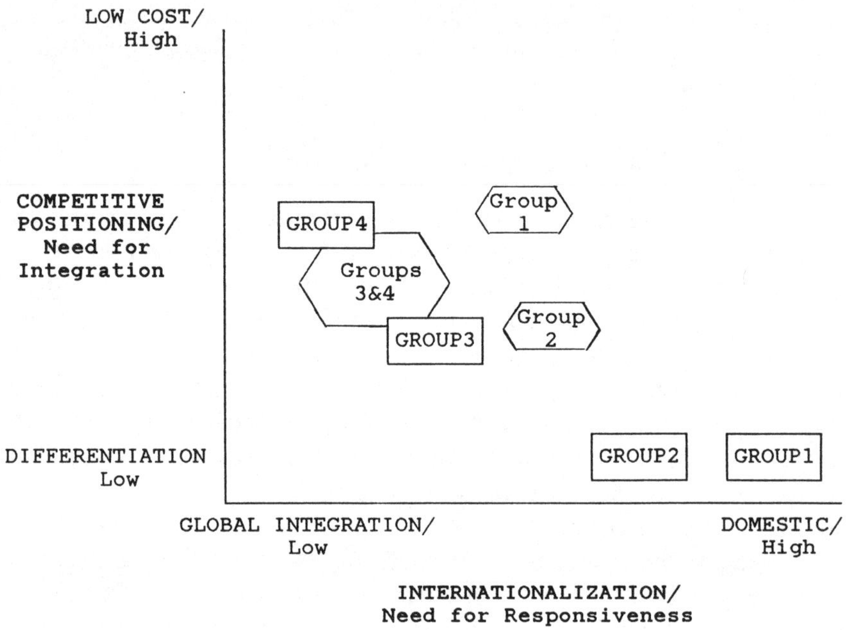

Group 1--Domestic, Product Specialization

Group 2--Exporting, High-Quality Offerings

Group 3--International, Product Innovation

Group 4--Global, Combination
--Complex Innovation
--Marketing Differentiation

to varying degrees by Groups 1 and 2, fairly tight matches were apparent between composite strategies and environmental perceptions involving Groups 3 and 4. In the case of Group 4, the match was particularly close, with few pressures for local responsiveness and moderate pressures for global integration being met with "global, combination" strategies designed to meet these contingencies. The match was perhaps less ideal for Group 3 businesses. These businesses perceived industry pressures as demanding more global integration and less local responsiveness than evidenced by their strategic behavior.

PERFORMANCE AND STRATEGY GROUPS: THE IMPORTANCE OF FIT

The consequences of matches and mismatches between environmental pressures and patterns of strategic behavior have been the subject of considerable research.[11] Much of this research has focused on the relationship between the match or fit established between environmental pressures and strategic behavior. As suggested, the performance implications of good fit are observed in positive business performance; poor fit, in turn, results in inferior performance.

Performance results reported in Figure 4.8 appear to demonstrate the consequences of poor fit between industry pressures and patterns of strategic behavior. In terms of *return on assets*, Group 4 businesses (global, combination strategy) significantly ($p > 0.05$) outperformed the three strategic groups. Compared with the top three-performing groups, Group 1 businesses (domestic, product specialization) had the worst performance levels. In terms of *return on investment*, Group 3 businesses (international, product innovation) significantly ($p > 0.10$) outperformed businesses from the remaining three strategy groups. Again, Group 1 had significantly poorer performance levels than the other three groups. In terms of *sales growth*, although no significant differences existed among the groups, the same pattern of superior performance for Groups 3 and 4 was evident. Again, these performance differentials are best explained in terms of fit between perceptions of industry pressures and strategic behavior.

Performance and Internationalization

Interestingly, these same performance measures may also indicate that those groups with the highest levels of international activity also have the highest performance levels (that is, Groups 3 and 4). Several researchers have suggested that the observed correlation between internationalization and performance is caused simply by the increased international exposure of businesses to environmental variance and risk.[12] This risk is then compensated through higher returns demanded by investors. From this perspective, international business is inherently riskier than simply domestic business, and businesses would not engage in international activities if not rewarded in a commensurate manner.

If this were the only aspect of risk from an internationalization perspective, there would be reason to support the suggested causal relationship between internationalization and performance. However, it has also been argued that instead of increasing risk, internationalization can actually reduce risk through portfolio diversification. By investing in a variety of countries, businesses can average out systematic risk and thus reduce overall risk.[13] From this perspective, businesses would still engage in international activities even when this results in lower performance because of the offsetting risk reduction stemming from diversification.

The extent to which both portfolio risk and exposure risk are able to offset each other has been discussed but not yet resolved in the literature. Methodological problems have made the systematic examination of the trade-off particularly problematic. One study by Rugman, Lecraw, and Booth, for example, found that "no evidence of excess profitability" was observed for a sample of large MNCs versus similar-sized domestic firms.[14] However, these researchers also failed to examine the relationship between the degree of international activity and profitability. Another study by Geringer, Beamish, and daCosta showed that the degree of internationalization *alone* is insufficient to explain MNC performance differentials.[15] Thus, while both forces are seen offsetting each other, little evidence is available to indicate how the balance in the trade-off will actually be determined.

The present study has shown that internationalization is correlated with performance, suggesting that portfolio risk may not completely compensate for exposure risk. Caution, however, is warranted in too quickly imputing causality in these relationships. Groose warns that methodological problems limit any generalizability of identified correlations between performance levels and levels of international activity.[16] The problem rests not only with assessments of risk but with performance as well. A fundamental challenge with studying international performance is that non-arms-length transfer pricing—caused by unequal taxes, exchange risk management, and so on—may distort the accurate assessments of profitability of international activities.[17] Thus, the relationship between internationalization and performance may not in fact be categorical.

Although this study does show a linkage between internationalization and performance, not enough support is available to confirm that changing internationalization alone will necessarily alter performance. Indeed, the evidence from this study could just as easily be interpreted as suggesting that the more *competitive positioning* emphasizes low cost, the higher the performance, irrespective of internationalization.

In this study, performance has been associated with groups of businesses that emphasize *both* internationalization and competitive positioning, and to draw conclusions by focusing on only one dimension would be improper. As a consequence, it is suggested here that performance should be more broadly studied by examining the relationship between both competitive positioning and internationalization as they interact with a broad array of environmental pressures. This necessarily returns the discussion of performance relationships to an examination of overall fit between business strategy and industry environment. Driven by perceptions of environmental pressures, internationalization and competitive positioning together determine fit and thus performance.

SUMMARY

An attempt was made to extend the present study by relating the composite strategies of businesses with perceptions of environmental imperatives regarded as triggers of globalization. Here, it was found that businesses pursuing "domestic, product specialization" and "exporting, high-quality offerings" composite strategies exhibited poor fit between strategic behavior and environmental pressures. Performance aspects of this poor fit were examined. It was evident that performance differentials separated strategy groups and that these differentials, as identified, could be traced to dissimilar patterns of strategic behavior. Using three objective measures of performance, three broad trends were evident: (1) Groups 3 and 4 were the highest-performing groups, (2) Group 1 was the lowest-performing group, and (3) Group 2 had middle-performance levels.

NOTES

1. See Hofer (1975), Hofer and Schendel (1978), Ginsberg and Venkatraman (1985), and Andrews (1987).

2. By appealing to the strategic management perspective of decision making, it is recognized that the causality suggested by the traditional Bain/Mason perspective of Industrial Organization (IO) (namely, the irrevocable influence industry membership has on performance) can indeed be bidirectional (Porter, 1981). The result is that fit is dependent on strategic behavior that is contingent on, but not determined solely by, industry pressures. As a consequence, strategic groups can potentially emerge with different performance levels within the same industry. These performance differentials would result from different and sometimes misplaced perceptions of industry pressures.

3. Prahalad and Doz (1987) are unfortunately not specific with respect to what constitutes "performance" in an international framework. The notion that the viability of strategies is dependent on the proper alignment of businesses with their respective contexts is also explicitly supported by Porter (1986b), Leontiades (1986), and Ghoshal (1987).

4. Prescott (1983), Prahalad and Doz (1987), Murray (1988), and C. Hill (1988).

5. The notion that perceptual environments may not coincide with actual environments has been discussed by Duncan (1972), Downey, Hellriegel, and Slocum (1975), Hambrick and Snow (1977), Weick (1979), and Bourgeois (1980b), among others. Although little agreement exists over the relative salience of perceived versus objective environments, support for their differentiation has emerged. Furthermore, perceptual environments have been regarded as "crucial inputs to the strategy-making process" (Bourgeois, 1980b: 35). Thus, while perceptual environments may not be representative of actual environments, evidence suggests that strategy formulation is based on the perceived environment.

6. Drucker (1980) and McGee and Thomas (1988).

7. McGee and Thomas (1988: 54).

8. See, for example, Vernon (1979), Cvar (1984), Hout, Porter, and Rudden (1982), Hamel and Prahalad (1985), Ohmae (1985), Kogut (1985b), Porter (1986a), Ghemawat and Spence (1986), Doz (1986, 1987), Ghoshal (1987), Jolly (1988), and McGee and Thomas (1988).

9. See Doz (1980, 1987), Hout, Porter, and Rudden (1982), Cvar (1984), Porter (1986a), and Bartlett and Ghoshal (1987b).

10. Prahalad and Doz (1987).

11. Hofer (1975), Miller and Friesen (1978), Miles and Snow (1984), Venkatraman and Camillus (1984), Porter (1985), Lorange, Scott-Morton, and Ghoshal (1986).

12. For a more complete discussion of this perspective, see Naumann-Etienne (1974), Shapiro (1978), and Root (1987).

13. See Ragazzi (1973), Solnik (1974), and Lessard (1983) for a more complete discussion.

14. Rugman, Lecraw, and Booth (1985: 136).

15. Geringer, Beamish, and daCosta (1989: 117) conclude that both diversification strategy and degree of internationalization influence performance. This conclusion is further caveated by the notion that the performance benefits of internationalization diminish beyond some "threshold" limit and that the implementation of a particular strategy plays an important role in determining performance levels.

16. Grosse (1981).

17. Lall (1973) and Choi and Czechowicz (1983).

CHAPTER 7

CONCLUSIONS AND IMPLICATIONS

The purpose of this chapter is to summarize the findings of this study and to suggest several implications for practicing managers. Many of the comments are prescriptive in nature and act to extend the existing results to broader issues of U.S. international competitiveness. As such, the discussion may also be of interest to both academic researchers and policymakers.

The chapter is divided into four main sections. The first section provides a brief summary of the study's methodology and findings. From this review, three main themes emerge that are the subject of further discussion: namely, (1) the heightened role of quality in determining competitive advantage; (2) the increased regionalization of competition; and (3) the viability of a number of alternate strategies for U.S. businesses in global industries. These themes will be addressed in the second, third, and fourth sections of the chapter.

SUMMARY OF THE RESEARCH FINDINGS

Two overarching research questions served to drive this study: Do distinct patterns of strategic behavior exist for businesses that operate within global industries? and Which patterns of strategic behavior are associated with superior performance levels in global industries? In order to explore these questions, 11 four-digit SIC code industries were first identified using a three-stage process designed to uncover only the most "global" of industries. After isolating this set of global industries, medium and large businesses were identified using two different minimum-size criteria. The strategic behavior of these businesses was then determined using three distinct measurement sources: questionnaire data that were analyzed using principal components analysis, cluster analysis, and ANOVA; secondary data involving 17 different busineses; and finally, posttests involving in-depth interviews with top executives from nine different businesses.

In all, four different composite strategies were identified in global industries: (1) "domestic, product specialization," (2) "exporting, high-quality offerings," (3) "international, product innovation," and (4) "global, combination." Performance comparisons were made across these four groups. It was found that the highest-performing groups were the "international, product innovation" and "global, combination" groups; the lowest-performing group was the "domestic, product specialization" group, with middle-level performance levels being reported by the "exporting, high-quality offerings" group. With this foundation, the nature of the contingency fit between perceptions of industry pressures and patterns of strategic behavior was also examined.

The study revealed that U.S.-based global competitors do not pursue low-cost strategies, nor do they recognize the world as an undifferentiated global marketplace. While businesses recognized the transcendent pressures of globalization, the dominant competitive arena was regional, not global. Within these regional competitive environments, U.S.-based competitors overwhelmingly emphasized differentiation strategies, where competitive positioning was predominantly based on quality offerings. Quality was almost universally stressed as a necessary determinant of competitiveness. Another theme evident in the findings was the importance strategy-industry fit played in determining business unit performance. Here it was recognized that perceptions of industry pressures may be more important than the actual pressures in determining strategies and hence performance.

The themes of quality, regionalization, and missed industry opportunities have remained largely unexplored in the international strategic management literature. They are clearly topics that are ripe for further research, from both managerial and academic perspectives. The next three sections of the chapter are designed to extend the discussion of these themes. As such, the discussion goes beyond the current study's immediate findings to suggest a variety of implications for managers and researchers challenged by the competitive demands of the global environment.

QUALITY AND INTERNATIONAL COMPETITIVENESS

It is becoming increasingly clear that much of the focus of U.S. international competition is shifting in favor of producing high-quality goods and services. Throughout the early 1980s, lagging product quality was frequently cited as a major cause of the declining competitiveness and mounting trade deficits of a variety of U.S. industries.[1] With these rising deficits has come a growing resolve by business leaders in a variety of industries to improve product and service quality.[2] The end result is that quality is now a dominant element in the competitive positions of a wide variety of American manufacturing businesses.[3] Nowhere is this more true than in global industries.

Determinants of Quality

In its broadest sense, *quality* can be defined as that which conforms "to the specifications for the product or service as laid down by engineering and management."[4] While quality specifications are internally generated, they are without doubt driven by perceptions and values that are determined in the marketplace. Consequently, a strategy founded on providing consistent quality will essentially meet or exceed the quality expectations of customers.

Although quality ultimately involves the nature of the business's contact with its customers, providing high-quality offerings requires the concerted efforts of the entire business unit. Quality necessarily involves input from upstream and downstream activities. Here, the *value chain* provides the basic tool for analyzing quality offerings.[5] Using this framework, each activity along the value chain serves as a potential site for adding and influencing quality. Quality can be the focus of a host of value activities including basic manufacturing, assembly, product transportation, marketing and sales, service, and a variety of support activities including raw material procurement, human resource management, and research and development. Each of these activities can be manipulated to add quality to the final product delivered to the customer. In order to make significant improvements in the degree of quality offerings a business is able to provide, it is often necessary that the business leverage the capabilities of its entire value chain. Attention to manufacturing or marketing quality alone is rarely enough from a competitive perspective.

As an example, one of the businesses involved in this study was seeing its international market share slowly being eroded by higher-quality foreign—principally Japanese—competitors. In 1981, an ambitious drive for a tenfold improvement in product and service quality was launched. The thought was that within five years the objective would be met and the business would be at a competitive advantage in the industry. By 1986, the business's objective for quality improvement was indeed achieved; unfortunately, its competitors had pursued similar quality improvement strategies. In response, the business adopted an even more ambitious "six sigma" quality improvement objective. *Six sigma* relates to defect rates as measured in standard deviations and has been applied to every step along the value chain. It was felt that only by linking product design, process design, scheduling, manufacturing, distribution, and sales could this objective be met. It makes little sense to promote service quality without first delivering reliable products to customers.

Quality in Relation to Cost and Differentiation

In emphasizing quality, a business is not forced to abandon other competitive positioning strategy types. Indeed, quality is compatible with both cost and differentiation. What this study found was that although quality is a driving force behind competition, it is rarely sufficient in and of itself to determine competitive advantage in global industries.

Quality and Differentiation. Quality is clearly a relative construct. While all businesses may emphasize quality, some may select a strategy based on further differentiating their offerings according to the quality of the products and services they provide. Indeed, in this study one of the dominant competitive positioning strategy types identified was "high-quality offerings." Here, the emphasis on quality permeated every activity along the value chain; quality was clearly the overriding determinant of competitive positioning. Yet, in a separate example, other businesses emphasized high-quality offerings as a necessary characteristic of competing in a global industry while concurrently seeking to differentiate themselves according to product specialization or technological innovation. In these cases, quality dominated competitive positioning but did not differentiate businesses in global industries. Here, quality was consistent with both innovation and specialization. No trade-offs were mandated.

Quality and Cost. A business's emphasis on high-quality offerings also has important implications for its cost structure. Conventional wisdom suggests that low cost is incompatible with high quality and that a business's competitive position would be compromised by concurrently pursuing both. Using this reasoning, it would not be surprising that faced with high comparative costs at home, U.S. businesses would have a greater propensity to pursue competitive positioning strategies based on high-quality offerings. In this case, high U.S. costs would appear to encourage indigenous businesses to differentiate themselves in ways that discount the cost advantages of international competitors.

Two arguments challenge this conventional wisdom. The first argument suggests that high quality may indeed be compatible with low costs. Supporting this argument is the tight linkage that exists between quality and productivity, which is itself directly tied to costs. "Quality" in this sense "is productivity, because so many costs—rework, scrap, inspection, customer returns, and so forth—are avoided each time a quality improvement is effected."[6] Empirical evidence also seems to support the argument that in the long run costs will be reduced if businesses concentrate on quality improvements.[7] Consequently, given the close linkages between costs and quality, businesses may find that quality is a necessary element in a low-cost strategy.

As a separate yet related point, it may be erroneous to assume that the United States is an inherently high-cost national base for conducting operations. This is important because if the United States represented a low- or moderate-cost base, many of the supposed imperatives for emphasizing quality would be eliminated.

High U.S. costs have most frequently been associated with labor rates.[8] Indeed, compared with many developing countries, U.S. labor costs often appear staggering. This is important insofar as global competitors have the capacity to exploit low labor cost opportunities by shifting production away from the United States.

In spite of clear direct labor cost differentials, high-cost U.S. labor represents an increasingly small portion of the total cost of making a product in the United States. Indeed, one study suggested that labor costs in the U.S. electronics industry (partially represented in this study) accounted for between 5 and 10 percent of total costs.[9] Using capital-intensive production processes, American workers also enjoy higher productivity than their counterparts in developing countries. Furthermore, the nature of the global imperative suggests that businesses can avoid home country cost disadvantage by leveraging low-cost alternative locations for the majority of value activities.

Although U.S. direct labor costs are significantly higher than costs in other—particularly developing—nations, the impact of these costs on final product costs is mixed. Productivity differentials, rework costs, transportation costs, and tariffs all impact final costs. Furthermore, the United States may provide a clear and offsetting competitive advantage in other dimensions affecting cost structure, such as land and capital. Thus, U.S. businesses are not forced to focus on high-quality (high-price) output because of any inherent cost disadvantages. Rather, quality is becoming an increasingly important requirement of international competition—irrespective of value activity location.

THE REGIONALIZATION OF COMPETITION

International strategic management research has been largely preoccupied with developing bipolar frameworks of international competition. As discussed in Chapter 5, these frameworks include measures of competitive positioning in terms of cost versus differentiation and measures of internationalization according to global versus (multi-) domestic strategies. The advantage of using bipolar frameworks is that they facilitate the structuring of a cluttered and often confusing set of activities—both external and internal to the organization. Another contribution of the frameworks is their utility in prioritizing the parameters and interactive effects of competition, albeit along only a limited number of dimensions.

Although two-dimensional frameworks have served strategic management researchers and practitioners well, they are far from ideal. Nowhere is this more true than with internationalization where a business's strategy is articulated along the domestic/global continuum. According to the frameworks, a business is either domestic or international; the critical issue becomes the degree of internationalization.

Problems with dichotomizing international competition are beginning to mount. Nowhere is this better seen than in Bartlett and Ghoshal's efforts to identify a new type of competition, one that they refer to as the "transnational solution."[10] The transnational strategy represents an attempt to add depth to the domestic/global dichotomy by suggesting the concurrent pursuance of multinational, international, and global strategies. Businesses facing the divergent pressures of domestic responsiveness, global integration, and worldwide innovation can respond in kind by building an internationally horizontal organization that facilitates the simultaneous pursuance of all three imperatives.

The posited transnational strategy represents a powerful attempt to fill a gap in the current literature in the area of mixed strategies. The gap exists because the commonly used 2 × 2 matrixes focus best on the extremes of either industry imperatives or strategic responses. Multifocal or international strategies are difficult to represent meaningfully in a two-dimensional framework because they deal with partial pressures or responses. What Bartlett and Ghoshal attempt to do is to change the way we look at the framework. Instead of partial pressures or responses, we have a combination of complete yet countervailing pressures that act to offset each other. The effect is powerful in that businesses are able to remain locally responsive while responding to pressures to integrate operations globally. As such, the transnational strategy has been proposed as a sort of middle-ground solution that, depending on the interpretation, may include regional strategies.

Unfortunately, the transnational solution may not be appropriate for all businesses. Although Bartlett and Ghoshal have held the transnational strategy up as the model for "major worldwide players," they also recognize that it is currently only a hypothetical solution and one that "does not correspond to any specific company."[11] In relation to this study's findings, a transnational strategy may be suggestive of a solution to a set of imperatives that may be misinterpreted by businesses. The weakness here is the framework's loyalty to the dichotomous conceptualization of international competition. It is not so much the inclusion of internationalization as it is the failure to account for *all* nondomestic systemic imperatives. For regionally focused strategies this becomes a critical concern. Indeed, if dominant pressures are uniquely regional, then the nature of competition may be largely misunderstood.

As reported in this study, competitive pressures and strategic responses were much more regional than global in nature. Irrespective of composite strategy, U.S. competitors regarded the United States as preeminently important in matters of investment, product development, production, and market position. As shown in Figure 6.1, none of the strategy groups perceived industry pressures in as global a context as anticipated in the literature. This helps explain at least part of the reason why broad global integration strategies were not pursued among the businesses identified.

While regional pressures come from a variety of sources, the most important developments are in the formalization of trading blocks. In North America, the Canadian-U.S. Free Trade Agreement is having a far-reaching impact on the business environment. The Free Trade Agreement, signed on January 2, 1988, promises to remove all tariffs for a wide variety of industries by 1998. Although trade barriers will remain in place in the areas of agriculture, culture, and maritime-related industries, virtually every other industry will face liberalized trade. The suggestion is that international operations will become increasingly rationalized/integrated according to regional imperatives. This is being born out in the trade figures where almost 70 percent of Canadian-U.S. trade is now intrafirm.

Within the European Community, 1992 is looming as a pivotal year in the elimination of trade barriers among the 12 member nations. The goal of 1992, as specified in the 1987 Single European Act, is to sweep away the nontariff barriers that restrict the flow of goods, services, and capital throughout the trading block. The effects of Europe 1992 on indigenous businesses are expected to mirror those changes brought about by the Canadian-U.S. Free Trade Agreement and include (1) increased concentration of industry structures, (2) consolidation of cross-border and national mergers and alliances, and (3) rationalization of production facilities within the region.[12]

Without a doubt, the establishment of trading blocks encourages the development of regional competitive strategies. Indeed, the restructuring of business strategies has been a clear objective of many governments in instituting and supporting free trade associations. While some businesses end up as net losers under free trade, structural adjustments are intended to produce a net positive contribution to industry members from a consumer welfare perspective. In addition to consumers, governments are also motivated in establishing regional free trade as a means of encouraging the establishment of structural imperatives that will result in improved global business competitiveness.

In the evolution away from nationally protected economies, the establishment of regional imperatives can serve to both encourage and protect businesses in the transition to globalization. According to one executive of a major European competitor in the information technology industry:

> We have to compete globally, which means actually introducing products at the same time in markets around the world. . . . [Yet we also] need a single European market with common technical standards. Without it, we cannot achieve the optimum scale and the lower unit costs we need to be competitive worldwide.[13]

Based on this reasoning, regional strategies provide the primary determinant of competitive advantage. Here the evolution of global competition is determined according to transregional market share battles. In this sense, regionalization also can be viewed as an interim step in the globalization of competition. Paradoxically, while globalization provides the imperative behind regionalization, regionalization introduces a set of distinct opportunities and threats—in effect, a distinct competitive environment—in its own right.

In spite of the long-term trend toward globalization, managers should not miss out on the short- and medium-term opportunities to leverage competitive advantage on a regional basis. In leveraging their strengths, regional competitors must increasingly balance pressures for regional responsiveness with pressures for globalization. Here the national-global dichotomy that characterized internationalization in global industries is quickly being replaced by a new national-regional and regional-global perspective. Regional forces now represent a distinct pattern of "systemic" pressures separate from either national or global forces.[14] These systemic pressures (and corresponding strategic responses) do not correspond with concurrent transnational forces. Rather, they represent a unique set of pressures that facilitate but do not necessarily lead to the adoption of viable global business strategies.

As a consequence of regionalization pressures, domestic businesses are pressured to become more regionally integrated, whereas global businesses are encouraged to focus their efforts on regional competition. The trend is apparent in a wide variety of businesses competing in global industries. Indeed, according to a recent Conference Board study of global team building in 30 U.S. MNCs,

> companies are shifting up to regional businesses as a logical outgrowth of, say, the effect of EC developments on their country-by-country businesses. Other companies are shifting down to regional businesses, having found their global businesses too cumbersome or insensitive to specific market needs.[15]

Thus, depending on the internationalization strategy type pursued, the regionalization of competition can be viewed as providing either an incentive or disincentive to adopt more global strategies.

SELECTED ALTERNATIVES

Managerial perceptions of strong regional pressures are evidence that a large number of businesses competing in global industries make imprecise assessments of global industry opportunities and threats. Here it was found that the businesses that placed the lowest emphasis on internationalization also had the highest misperceptions of industry pressures of the four strategy groups. These groups, while competing in nonglobal segments of global industries, nevertheless recognized strong pressures to be less responsive and more integrated. Yet they did not seem to be responding to these very pressures they acknowledged.

These misperceptions were often paired with inconsistent perspectives of global industry pressures, irrespective of the degree of internationalization. For example, businesses in the "global, combination strategy" group perceived relatively low levels of globalized buyer needs but high levels of worldwide product information. Similarly, businesses in the "domestic, product specialization strategy" group recognized high levels of globalized buyer needs but low levels of standardized purchasing practices worldwide.

Global Industry Pressures in a State of Flux

Misperceptions and inconsistencies in identifying industry pressures are an indication of environmental uncertainty. While this uncertainty is characteristic of all international business environments, the absence of overwhelming and transcendent industry pressures is more representative of an emerging industry context.[16] Emerging industries are identified by the nonexistence of competitive rules and by ambiguous structural parameters and can clearly coincide with broader global industry contexts.[17]

Another indication of the emerging nature of U.S. global industries is the preoccupation that the four groups had on establishing international production and distribution networks rather than managing existing networks. This was particularly relevant for the global and international strategy groups. More emphasis was placed on selling existing products to whomever would buy them than was placed on developing global "commitment." The presence of a globally integrated chain of value activities suggests inherently higher levels of operational risk by demanding commitment to far-flung facilities upon which the performance of the entire business unit may rest. Such levels of global commitment were not found in this study.

This is not, of course, to suggest that industries such as oilfield equipment and watches should be viewed as emerging industries in the United States but that these industries should be viewed as emerging global industries. The presence of global competitive pressures is a relatively new phenomenon. Within emerging global industries, businesses are confronting rapidly changing pressures that will encourage more global integration and relatively less national responsiveness. This should result in shifts in patterns of strategic behavior as the forces that define global competition mature.

Altering Fit. Given that the nature of industry pressures will only shift with time from that of an emerging global to a mature global industry, real pressures facing particularly the "domestic, product specialization" and "exporting, high-quality offerings" strategy groups will increase the extent of misfit between strategic behavior and industry pressures. Consequently, it can be argued that many businesses in the "domestic, product specialization" and "exporting, high-quality offerings" strategy groups can significantly improve performance levels by increasing emphasis on low-cost and global integration strategies. Here the regional arena provides an ideal testing ground for these strategies.

In terms of performance, it would be impossible to indicate precisely which businesses should change their patterns of strategic behavior. It is only safe to say that performance levels for the entire strategy group will suffer if some member businesses do not change strategic behavior and that there is opportunity for businesses to achieve good strategy-industry matches by increasing emphasis on low-cost and global integration strategies.

As was the case with the "domestic, product specialization" and "exporting, high-quality offerings" groups, a critical question is whether broad industry pressures for global integration and regional responsiveness will result in a shrinkage of the size of segments now being occupied by the "international, product innovation" and "global, combination" strategy groups. As global industries shift from emerging to mature and as domestic and exporting businesses adopt more regional strategies, one would expect increasing concentration in this segment of the industry and consequently less "room" for existing U.S. businesses to pursue differentiation strategies based on a regional emphasis. Indeed, as the industry matures and pressures for global integration become more pervasive, many businesses in the "international, product innovation" and "global, combination" strategy groups will significantly improve performance levels by increasing emphasis on low-cost and global integration strategies. The implication here is that a significant number of businesses that currently pursue regional differentiation strategies can improve performance by leveraging existing competitive advantage *across* regional boundaries and adopting global, low-cost strategies.

Again, in terms of performance, it would be impossible to identify which particular businesses would improve performance by altering strategy. Rather, it is suggested that performance levels of businesses represented by the entire strategy group will suffer if some members do not adopt low-cost global integration strategies. Conversely, to the extent industry pressures present greater opportunities for low-cost global integration strategies, businesses adopting these patterns of strategic behavior will see performance improve.

Non-U.S. Business Strategies in Global Industries. In reviewing the relationship between perceptual environments and objective environments, it must be appreciated that this research effort has focused exclusively on U.S. business-level strategies in global industries. Using U.S. business as the unit of analysis, it was found that various differentiation and internationalization strategies typified strategic behavior. However, the nature of non-U.S. business-level strategies in global industries was not addressed.

While patterns of internationalization may transcend all competitors irrespective of home country ties, there is growing evidence that *low cost may indeed be an important factor in the competitive positioning of businesses with ties to non-U.S. home countries.* Both conceptual and empirical evidence are offered in support of this contention.

From a conceptual basis, it has been asserted by several scholars that as industry competition matures, attention shifts increasingly to low-cost competition. According to Vernon's product cycle hypothesis, for example, competitors initially face price inelastic demand, followed by increasing pressures to reduce costs/prices in establishing international operations.[18] Thus, as industries mature, differentiation strategies give way to low-cost strategies. This is an assertion broadly supported by Murray, who argues that as industries mature, differentiation strategies become "increasingly difficult" to maintain.[19] Thus, to the extent that non-U.S. global industries are more mature, pressures to pursue low-cost strategies may become more pronounced over time. This also suggests that while U.S. businesses are pursuing various differentiation competitive positioning strategies, many non-U.S. businesses may be currently pursuing low-cost strategies.

There is also empirical evidence that a growing number of non-American businesses may already be competing on the basis of cost. Reference here is made to a recently published study by Ferdows et al. involving 643 responses from Japanese businesses.[20] In this study, carried out over a three-year period, overwhelming evidence was found that Japanese competitive strategies were fundamentally based on low cost. As cited in the study's findings:

> The overall picture which emerges is that the Europeans and Americans seem to be striving for higher quality, while the Japanese are

> primarily seeking lower costs and flexibility. One interpretation of this picture is that the Americans and the Europeans are aiming at overcoming what they perceive to be the relative deficiencies of their manufacturing compared to the Japanese, whereas the Japanese, having been relatively successful in both quality and delivery management, are now aiming at developing a new competitive edge which combines flexibility with low cost manufacture. We think this a reasonable interpretation.[21]

The suggestion is that as competitive pressures mature, strategies will evolve along a sequence where the first priority is the production of quality goods and services. Reliability, cost, and flexibility will all follow as the foci of competition.

In reviewing both the conceptual and empirical evidence, it is asserted that U.S.-based industry pressures and accompanying patterns of strategic behavior are somewhat unique. Using the IR grid developed by Prahalad and Doz, the suggestion is that global industry pressures do exist and that some non-U.S. businesses are pursuing global integration, low-cost strategies represented in the upper-left quadrant of Figure 5.3.[22] To a degree, U.S. businesses remain vulnerable to the threats provided by non-U.S. competitors pursuing strategies that recognize global industry pressures that transcend unstable regional environments.

CONCLUDING REMARKS

Without a doubt, the study of business strategy content in global industries is complex. From the international strategic management literature it could be expected that strategic responses should match industry imperatives. In this study, however, it was shown that although *general* matches were the norm, considerable discrepancies were apparent. On a purely perceptual basis, these mismatches have the effect of minimizing many of the threats incumbent in competing in a global industry. On an objective basis, however, the strategies that U.S. businesses pursued left them vulnerable to a host of global competitive pressures. Such vulnerability will not change with the mass adoption of low-cost global integration strategies.

Clearly, global industry opportunities and threats are maturing. The regionalization of competition has been encouraged by governments as a means of accelerating strategic change in the face of globalization. The intent is that from a regional base, businesses will be able to strike out against global competitors more effectively. Ironically, regionalization must also be viewed as a possible reprieve from globalization where regional niche strategies may become increasingly viable. Here, political intent legitimizes competition and further encourages the convergence of industry pressures around not a global but a regional core. In the final analysis, businesses should respond on a case-by-case basis according to abilities to leverage existing competitive advantage.

NOTES

1. Krugman and Hatsopoulos (1987).
2. Dreyfuss (1988).
3. As an example of the pervasiveness of U.S. strategic emphasis on quality, in a recent three-year study involving 596 responses from U.S. manufacturing businesses, almost every U.S. manufacturer considered its ability to offer consistent quality to be of the highest importance in determining its ability to compete effectively (Ferdows et al., 1986: 9).
4. Schmenner (1984: 409).
5. The application of the value chain to quality analysis draws from Porter's (1985) work on the sources of competitive advantage.
6. Schonberger (1982: 81).
7. For example, Hayes and Wheelwright (1984) and Ferdows et al. (1986).
8. The role of labor costs in determining comparative advantage is the basis of the Hechscher-Olin theory, which focuses on the causes and direction of international trade. The Leontief "paradox," first published in 1953, provides a more detailed analysis of comparative advantage by looking at trade flows of capital-intensive goods. Here, specialized labor mitigates the importance of cost in determining production location. The identification of the U.S. comparative disadvantage in costs has been most frequently associated with labor and has been applied to various theories of the multinational enterprise. See, for example, Vernon (1966, 1979), Grosse (1981), and Calvet (1981).
9. See Ohmae (1985) and Markides and Berg (1988) for a discussion of the labor cost differentials involving the United States and other developed countries.
10. Bartlett and Ghoshal (1989).
11. See ibid., p. 16.
12. See External Affairs Canada (1989: 6–7).
13. Quote taken from the transcript of an interview with Wisse Dekker, chairman of the supervisory board of N. V. Philips, as reported by Stone (1989: 91).
14. Systemic forces in this regard represent the pattern of external political and market forces as well as intraindustry forces among the businesses competing within the region. This conceptualization of systemic pressures draws heavily from the work of Hoffmann (1961) and Kaplan (1964), who applied a systemic framework to the relations of nations. Using this framework, systemic pressures relate exclusively to industry structure pressures.
15. See Conference Board (1989: 13).
16. See McGee and Thomas (1988).
17. Porter (1980).

18. Vernon (1966).
19. Murray (1988).
20. See Ferdows et al. (1986).
21. Ibid., p. 9.
22. See Prahalad and Doz (1987) for a discussion of the IR grid.

CHAPTER 8

FUTURE DIRECTIONS

This study's findings represent the earliest stages in the development of a body of empirical research on competition in global industries. The principal ambition of the study was to derive a classification of business strategies with a recognition that "the primary objective of classification is to provide the foundation for all comparative studies." The findings of the classification, along with the research on the contextual and performance implications of fit, extend current conceptual and case research on global strategies and global industry contexts.

This study also provided an important synthesis of domestically oriented strategy content theory and more eclectic international business theory in developing a model of business strategy that facilitates the identification of patterns of strategic behavior irrespective of domestic or international contexts. The conceptualization of strategy according to a variety of sub-strategy constructs provides an excellent means to capture the multidimensional aspects of international competition. As such, this study represents the application of a holistic framework of business strategy. Such a framework can be used to further understanding of complex strategies in general and competition in global industries in particular.

LIMITATIONS AND FUTURE RESEARCH

Few research projects are without limitations, particularly when they focus on international topics. While the present study is determinate in its scope, it does suggest definite directions for future research, which, when more fully addressed in the future, will serve to advance much of the groundwork laid here.

Measurement Limitations

The research methodology employed in this study used three different data-gathering tools: a survey instrument, secondary data, and posttest interviews. Pretesting the survey instrument among multiple respondents within individual businesses was intended to maximize the comprehensiveness and validity of the measure. Participants were asked about the objectivity of the measures and whether they would suggest additional criteria than those found on the questionnaire. While this no doubt limited measurement problems in the final questionnaire, it clearly could not eliminate the possibility that some respondents may have been confronted with questions that were misinterpreted. To some extent this was mitigated by the option of not responding to particular questions. Here, no pattern of difficulties were observed. Space was also made at the end of the questionnaire for respondents to make additional comments. No pattern of comments was noticed here. Indeed, with few exceptions, responses typically encouraged further research while citing few difficulties with the survey instrument.

The secondary data and posttest interviews were designed to confirm and clarify the empirical classification. Ideally, secondary data and posttest interview data would have been gathered for all the businesses used in the classification. While every effort was made to expand the use of these data, a shortage of relevant and timely secondary sources combined with resource constraints prevented a greater reliance on posttest information.

Although posttest data were selected and compared in as objective a manner as possible, bias in measuring strategies through combining data sources is always possible. This would be particularly problematic when multiple data sources suggest conflicting patterns of strategic behavior. However, Snow and Hambrick argue that the subjectivity associated with sorting out conflicting information "will almost always be preferable to exclusive reliance on a single measurement method."[1]

Sample Bias

The focus of this study has been on the competitive patterns of U.S. businesses. The identification of patterns of strategic behavior by non-U.S. businesses was not addressed. As discussed in Chapters 2 and 5, global competition involves a globally integrated chain of value activities configured without regard to home nation pressures. As a consequence, the home location of global competitors should conceptually be inconsequential in a study of global competition. However, as was discussed in Chapter 7, home nation pressures are important in tempering perceptions of global industry pressures. This suggests the need for further research into non-U.S. business strategies in global industries. Further studies could have the impact of refining the entire conceptualization of competition in global industries.

Identifying Global Industries

The identification of global industries in this study was centered at the four-digit SIC code level. However, a major problem with identifying the industry at the four-digit level is that while two businesses may have the same four-digit SIC code, they may compete in entirely different five-digit industries.[2] As discussed in Chapters 2 and 3, this problem may be compounded by inconsistencies in the literature over identifying global industries according to a set number of SIC code digits. In order to circumvent this problem and provide continuity in identifying global industries, trade flow data were isolated at the four-digit level. No doubt, additional mechanisms could have been employed to control for globalness. The objective here was not to identify *all* global industries but to ensure that the industries selected met some reasonable criteria. It is left as a subject for further investigation whether the patterns of strategic behavior identified in this study would have varied, had a different set of global industries been selected.

Focus on the Business Unit

In discussing the level of analysis issue, it is important to note that the business unit served as the focus of competitive analysis. Indeed, the classification is designed to identify only business-level composite strategies. Focusing on the business unit level of analysis is consistent with a large body of strategic management literature that equates the domain of the business unit with its industry context, which in this study was the global industry. Consequently, to study competition in global industries is necessarily to study patterns of strategic behavior at the business unit level.

However, recent work by Prahalad and Doz raises important questions about the appropriateness of limiting the unit of analysis to the business unit.[3] In assailing strategic management's preoccupation with the business unit level of analysis, Prahalad and Doz assert that the time is ripe to reexamine the "adequacy of the methodology."[4] Instead of focusing on the business as the unit of analysis, the authors suggest that research be focused on "discrete business clusters" composed of related business units. While much of this suggestion can be accommodated through adjusting SIC code level of abstraction, the notion that global strategic control extends to the corporate level has only recently been explicitly recognized[5] and warrants further study.

The unit of analysis issue also has ramifications in terms of performance assessments that can be made. It should be acknowledged that stand-alone performance measures of business units "fail to reflect the strategic contribution of a business to competitive advantage for the whole corporation."[6] This may be particularly important in the case of businesses emphasizing the "global, combination" strategy and to a lesser extent the "international, product innovation" strategy as identified in this study. In these two groups, there is growing anecdotal evidence that businesses are increasingly relying heavily on sharing and cross-subsidizing value activities with other business units in the corporation. Consequently, performance assessments may improperly estimate the performance outcomes of pursuing a particular composite strategy.

Other Performance Concerns

Even in making broad statements about relative performance levels, caution is warranted. Performance measures were reported over a three-year period from the beginning of 1985 to the end of 1987. During the early part of this period the real exchange rate of the dollar peaked versus a broad basket of currencies.[7] Even through 1986 the dollar held generally constant or continued to appreciate against the currencies of some key trading partners including Canada, Taiwan, Hong Kong, Mexico, Brazil, and South Korea.[8] Indeed, according to Krugman and Baldwin, "The continuing depreciation of the currencies of Mexico, Brazil, and Argentina largely outweighed the rise of the yen and European currencies" in terms of improved trade flows.[9] Because of the strong U.S. dollar during this three-year period, the performance levels for exporters (particularly businesses emphasizing the "exporting, high-quality offerings" composite strategy) may well be negatively biased. In turn, strictly domestic competitors—businesses emphasizing the "domestic, product specialization" strategy—would benefit as higher-priced imports would result in less price competition at home and thus potentially higher performance levels.[10]

In broad terms, a recognition that financial performance measurements may not provide optimal assessments of effectiveness also has considerable support in a broad range of organizational literature.[11] Limiting measures of business unit "effectiveness" to objective market assessments of business unit performance is to assume that the alternative criteria are of secondary importance. Clearly, future research needs to explore other aspects of effectiveness in global competition.

Static Assessments of Strategy Content

The theoretical underpinnings of this study are built on the notion that organizations match their distinctive competencies with their competitive environments in pursuit of organizational goals. While this study has focused on the nature of the match obtained, no attempt was made to address systematically the process associated with achieving strategic fit. As such, this study is based on static assessments of realized strategy content. The composite strategies identified represent "actually implemented strategies."[12] No indication is made of the paths businesses have taken in arriving at current strategies. This is a problem that is endemic in the strategy formulation and contingency-based strategic management research.

The process aspect of strategic fit can itself take on two separate meanings: (1) the implementation associated with internally matching strategy content with aspects of the organization's structure and resources and (2) the process associated with formulating the strategy in the first place. Of the former, the intermediary role that implementation plays in transforming strategy content into performance has much support in the literature.[13] While this study has attempted to identify broad patterns of strategic behavior and then relate these patterns to levels of performance, it is recognized that strategy implementation plays a vital role in making this linkage a reality. In this study, performance appraisals were based on one-time appraisals of fit. By failing to study the dynamic relationships between strategic behavior and changing industry pressures, no assertions can be made that present levels of fit will continue in the future. To date, no known empirical research has been conducted that attempts to classify the nature of strategy formulation and implementation linkages in global industries in either a static or dynamic context. Clearly, this is fertile ground for future research.

The second aspect of strategy process that provides perhaps the most interesting area for future research centers on the role top managers play in formulating global strategies. Much has been said about the importance environmental perceptions play in strategy formulation. It has been shown that either top managers misperceive global industry pressures or fail to perceive the extent of global pressures that dominate some segments of the industry. Time and again in the interview stage of the classification process in this study, it was acknowledged that managerial preoccupation with U.S. markets and general unfamiliarity with international markets and opportunities were critical in *preventing* the adoption of more typically "global" strategies. The international cross subsidization of markets that conceptually typifies global strategies requires vision and commitment, which were often lacking in the businesses studied.

This finding that global strategies may be highly dependent on management skills and interests is supported by Doz and Prahalad, who argue

> that quality of management—providing the ability to conceive and implement complex and differentiated strategies in the context of a large diversified multinational company (MNC)—is likely to become an increasing source of competitive advantage between global competitors.[14]

A major reason for this finding is the belief that, until the present, global competition has been an emerging phenomenon. Markets have been able to support a mismatch of strategies. However, as global industry pressures evolve, U.S. management will face greater challenges—both in formulating and, perhaps more importantly, in implementing strategies built on vast networks of integrated value activities that with time will come to typify global competition more completely. In the end, it is management that will largely determine the nature of competition in global industries.

A Universal Model of Strategy Content

Finally, it is recognized that the model used in this study to capture competitive positioning and internationalization has not yet been tested in a strictly domestic context. While the more conventional, domestically focused strategy classification research seems to have been preoccupied with competitive positioning, it should be recognized that U.S. businesses, whether in global industires or not, are increasingly subjected to international competitive pressures. In ever greater numbers, strategy researchers will be required to broaden the scope of their investigations to include the internationalization dimensions of strategic behavior. Ideally, the ambition would be the application of the more comprehensive model of business strategy content suggested in this study to strategic management research in a broad spectrum of possible contexts, whether domestic, international, or global.

NOTES

1. Snow and Hambrick (1980: 537).
2. See Dess (1988) for a more complete discussion of this unit of analysis problem.
3. Prahalad and Doz (1987).
4. Ibid., p. 65.
5. Bartlett (1986) and Jolly (1988).
6. Prahalad and Doz (1987: 240). See also Gupta and Govindarajan (1986).
7. Krugman and Baldwin (1987).
8. Glick and Trehan (1986).
9. Krugman and Baldwin (1987: 9).
10. It is important to note that significant volumes of both inter- and intrabusiness unit imports and exports typified businesses in both the "international, product innovation" and "global, combination" strategic groups. The impact of the strong U.S. dollar on the performance levels of businesses in these two strategic groups is largely indeterminate.
11. Barnard (1938), Andrews (1971), Vancil (1976), R. Hall (1977), D. Katz and Kahn (1978), Cameron and Whetten (1983), and Cameron (1986).
12. Bourgeois (1980b).
13. D. Hall and Saias (1980), Gupta and Govindarajan (1984), Bourgeois and Brodwin (1984), and J. Galbraith and Kazanjian (1986).
14. Doz and Prahalad (1988: 347).

Appendix A
Survey Instrument

SECTION I: This section asks questions about the industry in which your business competes

Q1 An important part of understanding international competition is to understand the competitive dynamics within your industry. Considering only the sector(s) of the industry in which your business competes, indicate how characteristic each of the following statements are in describing your industry (circle number):

	not at all characteristic				extremely characteristic
1. BUYER / CUSTOMER NEEDS ARE STANDARDIZED WORDWIDE	1	2	3	4	5
2. STANDARDIZED PURCHASING PRACTICES EXIST WORLDWIDE	1	2	3	4	5
3. COMPETITORS EXIST THAT HAVE A PRESENCE IN ALL KEY MARKETS	1	2	3	4	5
4. DOMESTIC COMPETITION IS INTENSE	1	2	3	4	5
5. INTERNATIONAL COMPETITION IS INTENSE	1	2	3	4	5
6. DISTRIBUTION CHANNELS ARE HIGHLY CONCENTRATED WORLDWIDE	1	2	3	4	5
7. BUSINESS ACTIVITIES ARE SUSCEPTIBLE TO SCALE ECONOMIES	1	2	3	4	5
8. PRODUCT AWARENESS / INFORMATION EXISTS WORLDWIDE	1	2	3	4	5
9. INTERNATIONAL ACTIVITIES ARE RESTRAINED BY GOVERNMENTS	1	2	3	4	5
10. STANDARDIZED PRODUCT TECHNOLOGY EXISTS WORLDWIDE	1	2	3	4	5
11. TRANSPORTATION COST IS AN IMPORTANT ELEMENT IN FINAL COST	1	2	3	4	5
12. LOCAL CUSTOMER SERVICE IS REQUIRED IN ALL MARKETS	1	2	3	4	5
13. COMPETITORS MARKET A STANDARDIZED PRODUCT WORLDWIDE	1	2	3	4	5
14. FACTOR COSTS (wages, materials, capital) DIFFER SIGNIFICANTLY FROM COUNTRY TO COUNTRY	1	2	3	4	5

Q2 How often is it typical for your business and its primary competitors to instigate major changes in all or part of the line of products offered (circle number):

1 ANNUALLY (FOR EXAMPLE, ANNUAL MODEL CHANGES)
2 SEASONALLY
3 PERIODICALLY (BUT AT INTERVALS LONGER THAN 1 YEAR)
4 PERIODICALLY (BUT AT INTERVALS LESS THAN 1 YEAR)
5 NO REGULAR PERIODIC PATTERNS OF CHANGE

Q3 Given the current state of technology in the methods of production or in the products offered by your business and its major competitors, how long would it be before this technology is obsolete (circle number):

1 GREATER THAN TEN YEARS
2 BETWEEN 5 AND 10 YEARS
3 BETWEEN 2.5 AND 5 YEARS
4 BETWEEN 1 AND 2.5 YEARS
5 LESS THAN 1 YEAR

SECTION II: This section asks questions about your business, its objectives, strategies, and products

Q1 Your business is best described as (circle number):

1 CONSUMER-PRODUCTS MANUFACTURER
2 INDUSTRIAL / COMMERCIAL PRODUCTS MANUFACTURER
3 RETAIL / WHOLESALE DISTRIBUTOR

Q2 How would you describe the stage of development of the major product(s) sold by your business during the last three years (circle number):

1 **INTRODUCTORY STAGE:** primary demand for the product just starting to grow; products still unfamilar to many potential buyers

2 **GROWTH STAGE:** demand growing at 10 % or more annually in real terms, technology or competitive structure still changing

3 **MATURITY STAGE:** products familiar to vast majority of prospective users; technology and competitive structure reasonably stable

4 **DECLINE STAGE:** products viewed as commodities; weaker competitors beginning to exit

Q3 Indicate how characteristic each of the following objectives are to your business. Your objective is to maximize (circle number):

	not at all characteristic				extremely characteristic
1. NET PROFIT OVER FIVE YEARS	1	2	3	4	5
2. RATE OF GROWTH	1	2	3	4	5
3. MARKET SHARE	1	2	3	4	5
4. EMPLOYEE REWARDS AND BENEFITS	1	2	3	4	5
5. NET PROFIT OVER THE COMING YEAR	1	2	3	4	5
6. PENETRATION OF INTERNATIONAL MARKETS	1	2	3	4	5
7. INNOVATION	1	2	3	4	5
8. ASSETS AND RESERVES	1	2	3	4	5
9. DIVIDEND PAYOUT	1	2	3	4	5
10. PRICE LEADERSHIP	1	2	3	4	5
11. SERVICE TO COMMUNITY	1	2	3	4	5
12. EQUIPMENT AND PLANT MODERNESS	1	2	3	4	5
13. PRODUCTIVITY (OUTPUT PER EMPLOYEE)	1	2	3	4	5

Q4 Listed below are various competitive methods that might be important to competing in your industry. Indicate how important each item is to the current strategy of your business (circle number):

	not at all important						extremely important
1. PROMOTE NEW PRODUCT DEVELOPMENT	1	2	3	4	5	6	7
2. TIGHTLY CONTROL OVERHEAD & VARIABLE COSTS	1	2	3	4	5	6	7
3. BUILD BRAND IDENTIFICATION	1	2	3	4	5	6	7
4. EMPHASIZE CUSTOMER SERVICE / SERVICE QUALITY	1	2	3	4	5	6	7
5. SERVE A WIDE VARIETY OF CUSTOMERS	1	2	3	4	5	6	7
6. PROMOTE INNOVATION IN MANUFACTURING PROCESSES	1	2	3	4	5	6	7
7. EMPHASIZE LOW COST PER UNIT	1	2	3	4	5	6	7
8. INFLUENCE / CONTROL CHANNELS OF DISTRIBUTION	1	2	3	4	5	6	7
9. EMPHASIZE PRODUCT QUALITY	1	2	3	4	5	6	7
10. OPERATE IN A WIDE RANGE OF GEOGRAPHIC MARKETS	1	2	3	4	5	6	7
11. DEVELOP ENGINEERING AND R&D EXPERTISE	1	2	3	4	5	6	7
12. DEVELOP INNOVATIVE MARKETING TECHNIQUES	1	2	3	4	5	6	7
13. PRICE AT OR BELOW COMPETITIVE PRICE LEVELS	1	2	3	4	5	6	7
14. OFFER A BROAD NUMBER OF PRODUCTS / SERVICES	1	2	3	4	5	6	7
15. MONITOR MARKET OPPORTUNITIES CONSTANTLY	1	2	3	4	5	6	7
16. EMPHASIZE HIGH CAPACITY UTILIZATION	1	2	3	4	5	6	7
17. EMPHASIZE ADVERTISING AND PROMOTION	1	2	3	4	5	6	7
18. DEVELOP UNIQUE PRODUCT FEATURES	1	2	3	4	5	6	7
19. EMPHASIZE SPECIALTY PRODUCTS	1	2	3	4	5	6	7
20. UTILIZE HIGHLY SKILLED LABOR	1	2	3	4	5	6	7
21. BUILD REPUTATION IN INDUSTRY	1	2	3	4	5	6	7
22. PRODUCE HIGH PRICED PRODUCTS FOR MARKET NICHES	1	2	3	4	5	6	7
23. EMPHASIZE MODERN PLANT AND EQUIPMENT	1	2	3	4	5	6	7
24. DEVELOP EFFICIENT MANUFACTURING PROCESS	1	2	3	4	5	6	7
25. UTILIZE HIGHLY SKILLED SALES FORCE / AGENTS	1	2	3	4	5	6	7

Q5 How often do customers typically purchase the products sold by your business? (circle number):

1 WEEKLY OR LESS
2 BETWEEN ONCE / WEEK AND ONCE / MONTH
3 BETWEEN ONCE / MONTH AND ONCE / 6 MONTHS
4 BETWEEN ONCE / 6 MONTHS AND ONCE / YEAR
5 LESS THAN ONCE / YEAR

Q6 How would you describe the basic manufacturing processes for the majority of the products offered by your business (circle number):

1 CUSTOM MANUFACTURING
2 SMALL BATCH
3 LARGE BATCH
4 MASS PRODUCTION
5 CONTINUOUS PROCESS

Q7 In the market served, how important are installation, repair, customer education, & other product related services provided to end users? (circle number):

1 NOT AT ALL IMPORTANT
2 OF SOME IMPORTANCE
3 IMPORTANT
4 EXTREMELY IMPORTANT

Q8 Listed below are various methods that might be important to competing internationally. How important is each item to the current strategy of your business? (circle number)

	not at all important						extremely important
1. INVEST IN COUNTRIES WITH LOW COSTS (eg. labor, raw material)	1	2	3	4	5	6	7
2. UTILIZE POLITICAL SKILLS TO LOBBY FOR FAVORABLE FOREIGN GOVERNMENT POLICIES (eg. % local content, offsets)	1	2	3	4	5	6	7
3. INTERNATIONALLY CONTROL THE MANUFACTURING CYCLE FROM RAW MATERIALS TO DISTRIBUTION OF FINISHED PRODUCT	1	2	3	4	5	6	7
4. CONTROL WITHIN THE ORGANIZATION THE INTERNATIONAL TRANSFER OF INTANGIBLE ASSETS (eg.skills / technology)	1	2	3	4	5	6	7
5. SOURCE CAPITAL FUNDS INTERNATIONALLY	1	2	3	4	5	6	7
6. USE INTERNATIONAL POLITICAL RISK FORECASTING	1	2	3	4	5	6	7
7. SECURE LONG TERM CONTRACTUAL AGREEMENTS WITH INTERNATIONAL BUYERS / SELLERS	1	2	3	4	5	6	7
8. INVEST IN COUNTRIES WHICH OFFER INVESTMENT INCENTIVES (eg. infrastructure support, tax holidays)	1	2	3	4	5	6	7
9. VERTICALLY INTEGRATE OPERATIONS WORLDWIDE	1	2	3	4	5	6	7
10. UTILIZE FORMAL INTERNATIONAL PRODUCTION SHARING AGREEMENTS WITH OUTSIDE FIRMS (licensing, joint ventures)	1	2	3	4	5	6	7
11. UTILIZE FORMAL INTERNATIONAL MARKETING AGREEMENTS WITH OUTSIDE FIRMS	1	2	3	4	5	6	7
12. UTILIZE FORMAL INTERNATIONAL R&D / TECHNOLOGY SHARING AGREEMENTS WITH OUTSIDE FIRMS	1	2	3	4	5	6	7
13. MINIMIZE TAX LIABILITIES THROUGH TRANSFER PRICING AND METHOD OF CASH REMITTANCE	1	2	3	4	5	6	7
14. SAFEGUARD OPERATIONS FROM FOREIGN INTERVENTION	1	2	3	4	5	6	7
15. HORIZONTALLY INTEGRATE OPERATIONS WORLDWIDE	1	2	3	4	5	6	7
16. DEVELOP EXTERNAL INTERNATIONAL INFORMATION NETWORKS	1	2	3	4	5	6	7
17. SECURE ASSISTANCE OF U.S. GOVERNMENT / AGENCIES IN PENETRATING FOREIGN MARKETS	1	2	3	4	5	6	7

SECTION III: This section asks for descriptive information about your business and its market

Q1 For the last fiscal year, please indicate your business's approximate:

_________ NUMBER OF FULL-TIME EMPLOYEES
_________ NUMBER OF COUNTRIES WITH SUBSIDIARIES / JOINT VENTURES

Q2 What is the approximate market share of the four largest competitors in your market (include this business if it is one of the four largest):

_______%

Q3 Of the total employees in this business (managerial & non-managerial, salaried and hourly), what percentage is unionized:

_______%

Q4 For the last fiscal year, please indicate this business's approximate:

_________ TOTAL SALES (IN U.S. $)
_________ TOTAL INTERNATIONAL SALES (IN U.S. $)
_________ FOREIGN OPERATING PROFIT AS % OF TOTAL PROFITS
_________ FOREIGN ASSETS AS % OF TOTAL ASSETS

Q5 The market in which this business competes can best be charaterized by (circle number):

1 a high rate of technological change, global scale economies, and internationally standardized product demand

2 a relatively slow pace of technological change, the need for a high level of responsiveness on a country by country basis, and products customized to meet local tastes and preferences

3 the demand for state of the art products in some national markets and older generation products in other national markets, relatively standardized demand for products by key customers, and emphasis on the staggered introduction of technology to different host countries

SECTION IV: This section asks questions about the performance of your business

Q1 Indicate the range which best describes the average performance of your business over the past three years (your responses will be kept strictly confidential):

1. After-tax return on total assets was (circle number):
   1 greater than 25%
   2 between 20% and 25%
   3 between 15% and 20%
   4 between 10% and 15%
   5 between 5% and 10%
   6 between 0% and 5%
   7 negative net return on total assets

2. After tax return on total investment was (circle number):
   1 greater than 25%
   2 between 20% and 25%
   3 between 15% and 20%
   4 between 10% and 15%
   5 between 5% and 10%
   6 between 0% and 5%
   7 negative net return on total investment

3. Annual increase in total sales was (circle number):
   1 greater than 25%
   2 between 20% and 25%
   3 between 15% and 20%
   4 between 10% and 15%
   5 between 5% and 10%
   6 between 0% and 5%
   7 negative net drop in sales

Q2 Indicate the category which you feel best estimates how your business's performance over the last three years compared to other firms in the industry (circle number):

	LOWEST 20%	LOWER 20%	MIDDLE 20%	NEXT 20%	TOP 20%
1. AFTER-TAX RETURN ON TOTAL ASSETS	1	2	3	4	5
2. AFTER TAX RETURN ON TOTAL INVESTMENT	1	2	3	4	5
3. ANNUAL INCREASE IN TOTAL SALES	1	2	3	4	5

Appendix B
SIC Code Industry Emphasis across Three Key Global Industry Parameters

DEPENDENT VARIABLE: COMPETITORS WITH A PRESENCE IN ALL KEY MARKETS

SOURCE	DF	SUM OF SQUARES	MEAN SQUARE	F-VALUE
MODEL	3	2.803	0.934	0.76
ERROR	107	130.873	1.223	
TOTAL	110	133.676		PR > F
				0.517

DEPENDENT VARIABLE: INTENSE INTERNATIONAL COMPETITION

SOURCE	DF	SUM OF SQUARES	MEAN SQUARE	F-VALUE
MODEL	3	2.233	0.744	.98
ERROR	107	81.353	0.760	
TOTAL	110	83.586		PR > F
				0.406

DEPENDENT VARIABLE: COMPETITORS MARKET STANDARDIZED PRODUCT WORLDWIDE

SOURCE	DF	SUM OF SQUARES	MEAN SQUARE	F-VALUE
MODEL	3	1.256	0.419	0.26
ERROR	108	173.851	1.610	
TOTAL	111	175.107		PR > F
				0.854

Appendix C
SIC Code Industry Emphasis across Strategy Variables[a]

STRATEGY VARIABLES

SIC INDUSTRY	NEW PRODUCT DEVELOPMENT	CONTROL COSTS	BRAND REPUTATION
2879	5.714	5.357	5.357
3532	4.500	5.917	5.250
3533	5.615	6.384	5.308
3552	6.400	5.400	5.800
3636	5.667	5.000	6.000
3651	5.667	5.778	5.000
3674	6.087	5.739	4.565
3693	6.333	5.667	5.167
3721	5.800	5.900	5.800
3724	4.714	5.143	5.143
3728	5.833	5.833	4.250
3873	7.000	7.000	7.000
F-VALUE	1.61	0.89	1.07

STRATEGY VARIABLES

SIC INDUSTRY	MANUFACTURING INNOVATION	CONTROL CHANNELS	PRODUCT QUALITY
2879	5.000	5.214	5.786
3532	4.500	4.250	6.417
3533	4.538	4.000	6.231
3552	5.000	4.800	6.400
3636	4.667	5.333	6.667
3651	4.444	4.333	6.444
3674	5.261	3.913	6.478
3693	5.167	5.167	6.667
3721	4.700	3.300	7.000
3724	5.000	3.428	6.429
3728	5.583	3.250	6.750
3873	3.000	5.000	7.000
F-VALUE	0.75	1.45	1.55

[a]* Significance of difference in strategy means, $p < 0.05$

STRATEGY VARIABLES

SIC INDUSTRY	INNOVATIVE MARKETING	LOW PRICE	MONITOR MARKET
2879	5.286	3.923	5.143
3532	4.250	4.909	4.917
3533	5.000	5.154	5.769
3552	5.200	4.200	6.000
3636	5.667	2.333	5.667
3651	5.333	4.111	4.778
3674	4.869	4.043	5.391
3693	6.167	4.833	5.500
3721	5.600	4.300	5.500
3724	4.714	4.571	5.143
3728	5.083	5.167	5.583
3873	7.000	5.000	7.000
F-VALUE	1.17	1.29	0.76

STRATEGY VARIABLES

SIC INDUSTRY	CAPACITY UTILIZATION	SPECIALTY PRODUCTS	SKILLED LABOR
2879	5.286	5.000	4.071
3532	5.000	4.000	4.833
3533	3.923	4.538	4.538
3552	4.600	4.200	4.200
3636	4.667	6.333	3.333
3651	4.444	4.000	3.556
3674	5.000	4.954	5.043
3693	4.333	5.000	3.667
3721	3.500	4.555	5.700
3724	3.714	4.857	5.286
3728	4.417	4.500	4.917
3873	3.000	7.000	3.000
F-VALUE	1.20	0.86	1.86

[a*] Significance of difference in strategy means, $p < 0.05$

STRATEGY VARIABLES

SIC INDUSTRY	INDUSTRY REPUTATION	HIGH PRICES	MODERN PLANT
2879	5.571	4.643	4.643
3532	6.167	4.917	4.750
3533	6.154	4.538	4.000
3552	6.800	6.000	4.800
3636	6.000	6.333	5.333
3651	5.889	5.000	4.556
3674	5.783	5.000	4.818
3693	6.000	4.333	4.667
3721	6.400	4.800	4.700
3724	5.714	4.571	4.143
3728	6.417	5.250	5.167
3873	7.000	5.000	7.000
F-VALUE	1.03	0.64	0.61

STRATEGY VARIABLES

SIC INDUSTRY	EFFICIENT MANUFACTURING	SKILLED SALES FORCE	LOW-COST COUNTRIES
2879	5.500	5.571	2.500
3532	5.417	6.333	3.167
3533	5.538	5.769	3.461
3552	5.800	6.200	2.400
3636	5.333	6.333	5.000
3651	5.222	5.222	5.667
3674	5.739	5.261	3.521
3693	5.667	6.500	3.333
3721	5.700	5.500	3.100
3724	5.571	5.000	2.500
3728	6.000	5.167	2.917
3873	7.000	7.000	7.000
F-VALUE	0.38	1.38	2.49*

* Significance of difference in strategy means, $p < 0.05$

STRATEGY VARIABLES

SIC INDUSTRY	LOBBY GOVERNMENTS	CONTROL MFG CYCLE	CONTROL INTANGIBLES
2879	3.786	3.714	4.286
3532	2.333	3.750	4.917
3533	4.462	3.538	4.615
3552	2.600	2.400	3.800
3636	3.667	4.000	3.667
3651	3.125	3.778	3.875
3674	2.957	3.217	4.217
3693	4.333	3.833	3.667
3721	4.900	2.400	3.600
3724	3.167	2.500	3.167
3728	3.667	3.500	4.250
3873	1.000	1.000	1.000
F-VALUE	2.07*	0.78	0.83

STRATEGY VARIABLES

SIC INDUSTRY	INTERNATIONAL CAPITAL	POLITICAL FORECASTING	L/T INT´L AGREEMENTS
2879	3.077	3.308	4.643
3532	3.750	3.000	3.667
3533	3.692	2.846	4.538
3552	3.400	3.200	3.800
3636	5.333	4.667	4.000
3651	3.286	2.625	3.500
3674	2.783	2.826	4.348
3693	3.500	2.500	3.167
3721	3.500	3.100	4.900
3724	2.833	3.500	4.500
3728	3.500	2.583	4.333
3873	1.000	1.000	4.000
F-VALUE	0.82	0.87	0.72

[a]* Significance of difference in strategy means, $p < 0.05$

STRATEGY VARIABLES

SIC INDUSTRY	INVESTMENT INCENTIVES	VERTICAL INTEGRATION	PRODUCTION AGREEMENTS
2879	4.071	3.500	4.286
3532	2.417	3.000	4.083
3533	3.615	4.154	3.615
3552	2.800	2.800	3.600
3636	2.667	3.667	4.667
3651	2.750	4.000	3.333
3674	3.652	3.956	3.783
3693	2.333	2.500	3.167
3721	2.667	2.600	4.700
3724	2.333	2.167	4.333
3728	2.833	2.917	4.167
3873	1.000	1.000	7.000
F-VALUE	1.42	1.72	0.81

STRATEGY VARIABLES

SIC INDUSTRY	MARKETING AGREEMENTS	R&D AGREEMENTS	MINIMIZE TAXES
2879	3.929	3.214	4.571
3532	3.667	2.417	3.833
3533	2.846	2.417	4.769
3552	3.800	2.800	3.800
3636	4.333	2.667	5.000
3651	3.375	2.625	4.125
3674	3.727	3.869	3.913
3693	3.000	3.167	5.000
3721	3.555	2.700	2.200
3724	4.167	3.167	3.500
3728	4.273	4.333	3.000
3873	4.000	1.000	1.000
F-VALUE	0.53	1.64	2.04*

** Significance of difference in strategy means, $p < 0.05$

STRATEGY VARIABLES

SIC INDUSTRY	SAFEGUARD OPERATIONS	HORIZONTAL INTEGRATION	INFORMT'N NETWORKS	GOV'T ASSISTANCE
2879	4.357	3.857	4.429	3.357
3532	3.167	3.333	3.583	3.000
3533	4.769	3.462	3.615	3.307
3552	5.000	2.750	5.000	4.200
3636	4.333	2.667	2.667	1.667
3651	4.000	3.375	4.000	2.375
3674	4.000	3.391	4.273	3.304
3693	4.167	3.500	4.167	2.667
3721	3.600	2.333	4.800	4.900
3724	4.333	2.833	3.667	3.167
3728	4.917	2.417	4.000	3.083
3873	1.000	4.000	4.000	1.000
F-VALUE	1.12	1.01	0.78	1.40

* Significance of difference in strategy means, $p < 0.05$

Appendix D
SIC Code Respondents per Cluster

SIC CODE FREQUENCY PERCENT ROW PCT COL PCT	CLUSTER 1	2	3	4	TOTAL
2879	4 3.57 30.77 9.30	0 0.00 0.00 0.00	8 7.14 61.64 20.51	1 0.89 7.69 9.09	13 11.60
3532	5 4.46 45.45 11.63	2 1.79 18.18 10.53	3 2.68 27.27 7.69	1 0.89 9.09 9.09	11 9.82
3533	4 3.57 33.33 9.30	5 4.46 41.67 26.32	3 2.68 25.00 7.69	0 0.00 0.00 0.00	12 10.71
3552	1 0.89 20.00 2.33	1 0.89 20.00 5.26	2 1.79 40.00 5.13	1 0.89 20.00 9.09	5 4.46
3636	2 1.79 66.67 4.65	0 0.00 0.00 0.00	1 0.89 33.33 2.56	0 0.00 0.00 0.00	3 2.68
3651	5 4.46 55.56 11.63	1 0.89 11.11 5.26	2 1.79 22.22 5.13	1 0.89 11.11 9.09	9 8.03
TOTAL	43 38.39	19 16.96	39 34.82	11 9.82	112 99.99

SIC CODE	CLUSTER				
FREQUENCY PERCENT ROW PCT COL PCT	1	2	3	4	TOTAL
3674	11 9.82 47.83 25.58	2 1.79 8.70 10.53	9 8.04 39.13 23.08	1 0.89 4.35 9.09	23 20.54
3693	2 1.79 33.33 4.65	1 0.89 16.67 5.26	2 1.79 33.33 5.13	1 0.89 16.67 9.09	6 5.36
3721	3 2.68 30.00 6.98	4 3.57 40.00 21.05	3 2.68 30.00 7.69	0 0.00 0.00 0.00	10 8.93
3724	2 1.79 28.57 4.65	1 0.89 14.29 5.26	2 1.79 28.57 5.13	2 1.79 28.57 18.18	7 6.26
3728	3 2.68 25.00 6.98	2 1.79 16.67 10.53	4 3.57 33.33 10.26	3 2.68 25.00 27.27	12 10.72
3873	1 0.89 100.00 2.33	0 0.00 0.00 0.00	0 0.00 0.00 0.00	0 0.00 0.00 0.00	1 0.89
TOTAL	43 38.39	19 16.96	39 34.82	11 9.82	112 99.99

CHI-SQUARE VALUE 29.888

PROBABILITY 0.623

BIBLIOGRAPHY

Aaker, D., and Day, G. (1986). The perils of high growth markets. *Strategic Management Journal*, 7, 409–421.

Abell, D. (1980). *Defining the Business: The Starting Point of Strategic Planning*. Englewood Cliffs, NJ: Prentice-Hall.

Aldenderfer, M., and Blashfield, R. (1984). *Cluster Analysis*. Beverly Hills, CA: Sage Publications.

Aldrich, H., McKelvey, B., and Ulrich, D. (1984). Design strategy from the population perspective. *Journal of Management*, 10, 67–86.

Allan, G., and Hammond, J. (1975a). A note of the Boston consulting group concept of competitive analysis and corporate strategy. Boston: Harvard Case Services, #9–175–175.

Allan, G., and Hammond, J. (1975b). Note on the use of experience curves in competitive decision making. Boston: Harvard Case Services, #9–175–174.

Allison, G. (1969). Conceptual models and the Cuban missile crisis. *American Political Science Review*, 63, 689–718.

Andrews, K. (1971). *The Concept of Corporate Strategy*. Homewood, IL: Richard D. Irwin.

Andrews, K. (1987). *The Concept of Corporate Strategy*, (3rd ed.). Homewood, IL: Richard D. Irwin.

Ansoff, I. (1965). *Corporate Strategy: An Analytic Approach to Business Policy for Growth and Expansion*. New York: McGraw-Hill.

Ansoff, I. (1969). Toward a strategic theory of the firm. In I. Ansoff (Ed.), *Business Strategy*. Baltimore: Penguin.

Arndt, J. (1983). The political economy paradigm: Foundation for theory building in marketing. *Journal of Marketing*, 47, 44–54.

Arnold, S. (1979). A test for clusters. *Journal of Marketing Research*, 16, 545–551.

Astley, G., and Fombrun, C. (1983). Collective strategy: Social ecology of organizational environments. *Academy of Management Review*, 8, 576–587.

Bain, J. (1968). *Industrial Organization*, (2nd ed.). New York: Wiley.

Barnard, C. (1938). *The Functions of the Executive*. Cambridge, MA: Harvard University Press.

Bartlett, C. (1983). MNCs: Get off the reorganization merry-go-round. *Harvard Business Review*, 61, 138–146.

Bartlett, C. (1985). Global competition and MNC managers. ICCH Note No. 0–385–287, Harvard Business School.

Bartlett, C. (1986). Building and managing the transnational: The new organizational challenge. In M. Porter (Ed.), *Competition in Global Industries*. Boston: Harvard Business School.

Bartlett, C., and Ghoshal, S. (1987a). Managing across borders: New strategic requirements. *Sloan Management Review*, Summer, 7–17.

Bartlett, C., and Ghoshal, S. (1987b). *Managing across Borders: The Transnational Solution*. Boston: Harvard Business School.

Bartlett, C., and Ghoshal, S. (1989). *Managing across Borders: The Transnational Solution*. Boston: Harvard Business School Press.

Beamish. P. (1985). The characteristics of joint ventures in developed and developing countries. *Columbia Journal of World Business*, 20, 13–20.

Beamish, P., and Banks, J. (1987). Equity joint ventures and the theory of the multinational enterprise. *Journal of International Business Studies*, Summer, 1–16.

Benson, J. (1975). The interorganizational network as a political economy. *Administrative Science Quarterly*, 20, 229–249.

Biggadike, E. (1979). *Corporate Diversification: Entry, Strategy, and Performance*. Boston: Harvard Business School.

Blake, D. (1981). How to get operating managers to manage public affairs in foreign subsidiaries. *Columbia Journal of World Business*, Spring, 61–67.

Blau, P. (1970). A formal theory of differentiation. *American Sociology Review*, 35, 201–218.

Boddewyn, J. (1986). International political strategy: A fourth "generic" strategy? Paper presented at the Academy of International Business annual meeting, London.

Bonoma, T. (1985). Case research in marketing: Opportunities, problems, and a process. *Journal of Marketing Research*, May, 199–208.

Bourgeois, L. (1980a). Performance and consensus. *Strategic Management Journal*, 1, 227–248.

Bourgeois, L. (1980b). Strategy and environment: A conceptual integration. *Academy of Management Review*, 5, 25–39.

Bourgeois, L. (1984). Strategic management and determinism. *Academy of Management Review*, 9, 586–596.

Bourgeois, L., and Brodwin, D. (1984). Strategic implementation: Five approaches to an elusive phenomenon. *Strategic Management Journal*, 5, 241–264.

Bower, J. (1986). *Managing the Resource Allocation Process*. Boston: Harvard Business School Press.

Buckley, P., and Casson, M. (1976). *The Future of the Multinational Enterprise*. London: MacMillan.

Buckley, P., and Casson, M. (1979). *The Future of the Multinational Enterprise*. London: Holmes and Mein.

Buckley, P., and Casson, M. (1981). The optimal timing of a foreign direct investment. *Economic Journal*, March, 75–87.

Buss, M. (1982). Managing international information systems. *Harvard Business Review*, Sept.-Oct., 153–162.

Buzzell, R. (1968). Can you standardize multinational marketing? *Harvard Business Review*, November/December, 102–113.

Buzzell, R., Gale, B., and Sultan, R. G. (1975). Market share: Key to profitability. *Harvard Business Review*, January/February, 97–106.

Calvet, A. (1981). A synthesis of foreign direct investment theories and theories of the multinational firm. *Journal of International Business Studies*, Spring/Summer, 43–59.

Cameron, K. (1986). Effectiveness as paradox: Consensus and conflict in conceptions of organizational effectiveness. *Management Science*, 32, 539–553.

Cameron, K., and Whetten, D. (1983). Some conclusions about organizational effectiveness. In K. Cameron and D. Whetten (Eds.), *Organizational Effectiveness*. New York: Academic Press.

Casson, M. (1986). *Multinationals and World Trade: Vertical Integration and the Division of Labour in World Industries*. Boston: Allen & Unwin.

Cattell, R. (1986). The scree test for the number of factors. *Multivariate Behavioral Research*, 1, 245–276.

Caves, R. (1974). Causes of direct investment: Foreign firms' shares in Canadian and United Kingdom manufacturing industries. *Review of Economics and Statistics*, 56, 279–293.

Caves, R. (1982). *Multinational Enterprise and Economic Analysis*. London: Cambridge University Press.

Caves, R., and Jones R. (1985). *World Trade and Payments*, (4th ed.). Boston: Little, Brown.

Chandler, A. (1962). *Strategy and Structure: Chapters in the History of American Industrial Enterprise*. Cambridge, MA: MIT Press.

Chandler, A. (1986). The evolution of modern global competition. In M. Porter (Ed.), *Competition in Global Industries*. Boston: Harvard Business School.

Child, J. (1972). Organizational structure, environment, and performance: The role of strategic choice. *Sociology*, 6, 1–22.

Child, J. (1979). Organizational growth. In S. Kerr (Ed.), *Organizational Behavior*. Columbus, OH: Grid Publishing.

Choi, F., and Czechowicz, I. (1983). Assessing foreign subsidiary performance: A multinational comparison. *Management International Review*, 23, 14–25.

Chrisman, J., Hofer, C., and Boulton, W. (1988). Toward a system for classifying business strategies. *Academy of Management Review*, 13, 413–428.

Christensen, C., Andrews, K., Bower, J., Hamermesh, R., and Porter, M. (1987). *Business Policy: Text and Cases*, (6th ed.). Homewood, IL: Irwin.

Cohen, S., and Zysman, J. (1987). Why manufacturing matters: The myth of the post-industrial economy. *California Management Review*, Spring, 9–26.

Conference Board. (1989). Building global teamwork for growth and survival. Research bulletin no. 228.

Crookell, H. (1984). Specialization and international competitiveness. *Business Quarterly*, Fall, 26–30.

Cvar, M. (1984). Competitive strategies in global industries. Ph.D. dissertation, Harvard Business School.

Cvar, M. (1986). Case studies in global competition: Patterns in success and failure. In M. Porter (Ed.), *Competition in Global Industries.* Boston: Harvard Business School.

Czinkota, M. (Ed.) (1982). *Export Management.* New York: Praeger.

Czinkota, M., and Ricks, D. (1981). Export assistance: Are we supporting the best programs? *Columbia Journal of World Businesses,* Summer, 73–78.

Daniels, J., Pitts, R., and Tretter, M. (1984). Strategy and structure of U.S. multinationals: An exploratory study. *Academy of Management Journal,* 27, 292–307.

Davidson, W., and Haspeslagh, P. (1982). Shaping a global product organization. *Harvard Business Review,* July/August, 125–132.

Davis, P. (1986). An analysis of industry forces, corporate strategy, and business strategy as factors explaining business unit performance. Ph.D. dissertation, University of South Carolina.

Denzim, N. (1978). *The Research Act: A Theoretical Introduction to Sociological Methods.* New York: McGraw-Hill.

Dess, G. (1987). Consensus on strategy formulation and organizational performance: Competitors in a fragmented industry. *Strategic Management Journal,* 8, 259–277.

Dess, G. (1988). Environment assessment and organizational performance: Methodological and conceptual issues. Paper presented at the Academy of Management annual meeting, Anaheim.

Dess, G., and Davis, P. (1984). Porter's (1980) generic strategies as determinants of strategic groups membership and organizational performance. *Academy of Management Journal,* 27, 467–488.

Dillman, D. (1978). *Mail and Telephone Surveys: The Total Design Method.* New York: John Wiley.

Dillon, W., and Goldstein, M. (1984). *Multivariate Analysis: Methods and Applications.* New York: John Wiley.

Douglas, S., and Rhee, D. (1987). Competitive strategies in international markets: Some generic types. Unpublished manuscript, New York University.

Downey, H., Hellriegel, D., and Slocum, W. (1975). Environmental uncertainty: The construct and its application. *Administrative Science Quarterly,* 20, 613–629.

Doz, Y. (1980). Strategic management in multinational companies. *Sloan Management Review,* Winter, 27–46.

Doz, Y. (1986). Government policies and global industries. In M. Porter (Ed.), *Competition in Global Industries.* Boston: Harvard Business School.

Doz, Y. (1987). International industries: Fragmentation versus globalization. In B. Guile and H. Brooks (Eds.), *Technology and Global Industry: Companies and Nations in the World Economy.* Washington, DC: National Academy Press.

Doz, Y., and Prahalad, C. (1980). How MNCs cope with host government demands. *Harvard Business Review,* March-April, 149–160.

Doz, Y., and Prahalad, C. (1988). Quality of management: An emerging source of global competitive advantage. In N. Hood and J. Vahlne (Eds.), *Strategies in Global Competition.* New York: Croom Helm.

Dreyfuss, J. (1988). Victory in the quality crusade. *Fortune,* October 10, 80–88.

Drucker, P. (1954). *The Practice of Management.* New York: Harper & Row.

Drucker, P. (1980). *Managing in Turbulent Times.* New York: Harper & Row.

Duncan, R. (1972). Characteristics of organizational environments and perceived environmental uncertainty. *Administrative Science Quarterly,* 17, 313–327.

Dunning, J. (1980). Toward an eclectic theory of international production: Some empirical tests. *Journal of International Business Studies*, Spring/Summer, 9–31.

Dunning, J. (1981). *International Production and the Multinational Enterprise*. London: George Allen & Unwin.

Emery, F., and Trist, E. (1965). The causal texture of organizational environments. *Human Relations*, 18, 21–32.

Encarnation, D., and Wells, L. (1986). Competitive strategies in global industries: A view from host governments. In M. Porter (Ed.), *Competition in Global Industries*. Boston: Harvard Business School.

External Affairs Canada. (1989). 1992 implications of a single European Market: Executive summary. Part 1, effects on Europe. Ottawa: Department of Supply and Services.

Fagre, N., and Wells, L. (1982). Bargaining power of multinationals and host governments. *Journal of International Business Studies*, Fall, 9–23.

Fayerweather, J. (1981). Four winning strategies for the international corporation. *Journal of Business Strategy*, Fall, 25–36.

Fayerweather, J. (1982). *International Business Strategy and Administration*, (2nd ed.). Cambridge, MA: Harper & Row.

Ferdows, K., Miller, J., Nakane, J., and Vollmann, T. (1986). Evolving global manufacturing strategies: Projections into the 1990s. *International Journal of Operations and Production Management*, 6, 6–16.

Flaherty, M. (1986). Coordinating international manufacturing and technology. In M. Porter (Ed.), *Competition in Global Industries*. Boston: Harvard Business School.

Flowers, E. (1975). Oligopolistic reaction in European direct investment in the United States. Ph.D. dissertation, Georgia State University.

Fry, E. (1980). *Financial Invasion of the U.S.A.: A Threat to American Society?* New York: McGraw-Hill.

Fry, J., and Killing, P. (1989). *Strategic Analysis and Action*. Scarborough, Ontario: Prentice-Hall.

Galbraith, C., and Kay, N. (1986). Towards a theory of multinational enterprise. *Journal of Economic Behavior and Organization*, 7, 3–19.

Galbraith, C., and Schendel, D. (1983). An empirical analysis of strategy types. *Strategic Management Journal*, 4, 153–173.

Galbraith, J., and Kazanjian, R. (1986). *Strategy Implementation: Structure, Systems and Process*, (2nd ed.). St. Paul, MN: West Publishing.

Gale, B. (1972). Market share and rate of return. *Review of Economics and Statistics*, November, 412–423.

Geringer, M., Beamish, P., and daCosta, R. (1989). Diversification strategy and internationalization: Implications for MNE performance. *Strategic Management Journal*, 10, 109–119.

Ghemawat, P. (1986). Sustainable advantage. *Harvard Business Review*, September-October, 53–58.

Ghemawat, P., Porter, M., and Rawlinson, R. (1986). Patterns of international coalition activity. In M. Porter (Ed.), *Competition in Global Industries*. Boston: Harvard Business School.

Ghemawat, P., and Spence, A. (1986). Modeling global competition. In M. Porter (Ed.), *Competition in Global Industries*. Boston: Harvard University School.

Ghoshal, S. (1987). Global strategy: An organizing framework. *Strategic Management Journal*, 8, 425–440.

Ginsberg, A., and Vankatraman, N. (1985). Contingency perspectives of organizational strategy: A critical review of the empirical research. *Academy of Management Review*, 10, 421–434.

Glick, R., and Trehan, B. (1986). The outlook for net exports. *Federal Reserve Bank of San Francisco, Weekly Letter*, September.

Glueck, W. (1972). Business policy: Reality and promise. *Academy of Management Proceedings*, 108–111.

Gomes-Casseras, B. (1985). Multinational ownership strategies. D.B.A. thesis, Harvard University.

Green, P., Frank, R., and Robinson, P. (1967). Cluster analysis in test market selection. *Management Science*, 13, B387–B400.

Grosse, R. (1981). The theory of foreign direct investment. *Essays in International Business*, December, 1–51.

Grubel, H. (1977). *International Economics*. Homewood, IL: Richard D. Irwin.

Gupta, A., and Govindarajan, V. (1984). Business unit strategy, managerial characteristics, and business unit effectiveness at strategy implementation. *Academy of Management Journal*, 27, 25–41.

Gupta, A., and Govindarajan, V. (1986). Resource sharing among SBUs: Strategic antecedents and administrative implications. *Academy of Management Journal*, 29, 695–714.

Hafbauer, G., and Erb, J. (1984). *Subsidies in International Trade*. Washington, DC: Institute for International Economics.

Hair, J., Anderson, R., and Tatham, R. (1987). *Multivariate Data Analysis*, (2nd ed.). New York: Macmillan.

Hall, D., and Saias, M. (1980). Strategy follows structure. *Strategic Management Journal*, 1, 149–163.

Hall, R. (1977). *Organizations: Structure and Process*. Englewood Cliffs, NJ: Prentice-Hall.

Hall, W. (1980). Survival strategies in a hostile environment. *Harvard Business Review*, September/October, 75–85.

Hambrick, D. (1980). Operationalizing the concept of business-level strategy in research. *Academy of Management Review*, 5, 567–575.

Hambrick, D. (1983a). An empirical typology of mature industrial-product environments. *Academy of Management Journal*, 26, 213–230.

Hambrick, D. (1983b). High profit strategies in mature capital goods industries: A contingency approach. *Academy of Management Journal*, 26, 687–707.

Hambrick, D. (1983c). Some tests of the effectiveness and functional attributes of Miles and Snow's strategy types. *Academy of Management Journal*, 26, 5–26.

Hambrick, D. (1984). Taxonomic approaches to studying strategy: Some conceptual and methodological issues. *Journal of Management*, 10, 27–41.

Hambrick, D., and Lei, D. (1985). Toward an empirical priorization of contingency variables for business strategy. *Academy of Management Journal*, 28, 763–788.

Hambrick, D., and Scheter, S. (1983). Turnaround strategies for mature industrial-product business units. *Academy of Management Journal*, 26, 231–248.

Hambrick, D., and Snow, C. (1977). A contextual model of strategic decision making in organizations. *Academy of Management Proceedings*, 108–112.

Hamel, G., and Prahalad, C. (1985). Do you really have a global strategy? *Harvard Business Review*, July/August, 139–148.

Hamel, G., and Prahalad, C. (1988). Creating global strategic capability. In N. Hood and J. Vahlne (Eds.), *Strategies in Global Competition*. New York: Croom Helm.

Hamel, G., and Prahalad, C. (1989). Strategic intent. *Harvard Business Review*, May/June, 63–76.

Hannan, M., and Freeman, J. (1977). The population ecology of organizations. *American Journal of Sociology*, 82, 929–964.

Harrigan, K. (1980). *Strategies for Declining Businesses*. Lexington, MA.: Lexington Books.

Harrigan, K. (1982). Exit decisions in mature industries. *Academy of Management Journal*, 25, 707–732.

Harrigan, K. (1983). Research methodologies for contingency approaches to business strategy. *Academy of Management Review*, 8, 398–405.

Harrigan, K. (1985a). An application of clustering for strategic group analysis. *Strategic Management Journal*, 6, 55–73.

Harrigan, K. (1985b). Vertical integration and corporate strategy. *Academy of Management Journal*, 28, 397–425.

Harrigan, K. (1986). Matching vertical integration strategies to competitive conditions. *Strategic Management Journal*, 7, 535–555.

Hartigan, J. (1975). *Clustering Algorithms*. New York: John Wiley.

Harvard Business Review. (1987). Competitiveness survey: HBR readers respond. *Harvard Business Review*, September/October, 8–11.

Hatten, K. (1979). Quantitative research methods in strategic management. In D. Schendel and C. Hofer (Eds.), *Strategic Management*. Boston: Little, Brown.

Hax, A. (1989). Building the firm of the future. *Sloan Management Review*, Spring, 75–82.

Hayes, R., and Clark, K. (1986). Why some factories are more productive than others. *Harvard Business Review*, September/October, 66–73.

Hayes, R., and Wheelwright, S. (1984). *Restoring Our Competitive Edge*. New York: Wiley.

Henderson, B. (1979). *Henderson on Corporate Strategy*. New York: Mentor Books.

Herbert, T. (1984). Strategy and multinational organization structure: An interorganizational relationships perspective. *Academy of Management Review*, 9, 259–271.

Herbert, T., and Deresky, H. (1987). Generic strategies: An empirical investigation of typology validity and strategy content. *Strategic Management Journal*, 8, 135–147.

Hill, C. (1988). Differentiation versus low cost or differentiation and low cost: A contingency framework. *Academy of Management Review*, 13, 401–412.

Hofer, C. (1975). Toward a contingency theory of business strategy. *Academy of Management Journal*, 18, 784–810.

Hofer, C., and Schendel, D. (1978). *Strategy Formulation: Analytical Concepts*. St. Paul, MN: West Publishing.

Hoffmann, S. (1961). International systems and international law. In S. Hoffmann (Ed.), *The State of War: Essays on the Theory and Practice of International Politics*. New York: Praeger.

Hood, N., and Young, S. (1979). *The Economics of Multinational Enterprise*. New York: Longman.

Hout, T., Porter, M., and Rudden, E. (1982). How global companies win out. *Harvard Business Review*, September/October, 98–108.

Hunt, M. (1972). Competition in the major home appliance industry, 1960–1979. Ph.D. dissertation, Harvard University.

Hunt, S. (1983). *Marketing Theory: The Philosophy of Marketing Science*. Homewood, IL: Irwin.

Hymer, S. (1970). The efficiency (contradiction) of multinational corporations. *American Economic Review*, 60, 441–448.

Jackson, J. (1980). Principal components and factor analysis: Part-1 principal components. *Journal of Quality Technology*, 12, 201–213.

Jick, T. (1979). Mixing qualitative and quantitative methods: Triangulation in action. *Administrative Science Quarterly*, 24, 602–611.

Johnson, H. (1970). The efficiency and welfare implications of the multinational corporation. In C. Kindleberger (Ed.), *The International Corporation: A Symposium*. Cambridge, MA: MIT Press.

Jolly, V. (1988). Global competitive strategies. In C. Snow (Ed.), *Strategy, Organization Design, and Human Resource Management*. Greenwich, CT: JAI Press.

Kaplan, M. (1964). *Systems and Process in International Politics*. New York: Wiley.

Katz, D., and Kahn, R. (1978). *The Social Psychology of Organizations*. New York: John Wiley & Sons.

Katz, R. (1970). *Cases and Concepts in Corporate Strategy*. Englewood Cliffs, NJ: Prentice-Hall.

Keegan, W. (1969). Multinational product planning: Strategic alternatives. *Journal of Marketing*, 33, 58–62.

Keels, K., Chrisman, J., Sandberg, W., and Schweiger, D. (1987). A causal model of industry fragmentation. Unpublished manuscript, University of South Carolina.

Killing, P. (1982). How to make a global joint venture work. *Harvard Business Review*, May/June, 120–127.

Kim, J., and Mueller, C. (1978). *Introduction to Factor Analysis*. Beverly Hills: Sage Publications.

Kindleberger, C. (1969). *American Business Abroad: Six Lectures on Direct Investment*. New Haven, CT: Yale University Press.

Kindleberger, C. (1984). *Multinational Excursions*. Cambridge, MA: MIT Press.

Korbin, S. (1982). *Managing Political Risk Assessment*. Berkeley: University of California Press.

Kogut, B. (1985a). Designing global strategies: Comparative and competitive value-added chains. *Sloan Management Review*, Summer, 15–28.

Kogut, B. (1985b). Designing global strategies: Profiting from operational flexibility. *Sloan Management Review*, Fall, 27–38.

Kotler, P. (1986). Megamarketing. *Harvard Business Review*, March/April, 117–124.

Krugman, P., and Baldwin, R. (1987). The persistence of the U.S. trade deficit. *Brookings Papers on Economic Activity*, 1, 1–43.

Krugman, P., and Hatsopoulos, G. (1987). The problem of U.S. competitiveness in manufacturing. *New England Economic Review*, January/February, 18–29.

Lall, S. (1973). Transfer-pricing by multinational manufacturing firms. *Oxford Bulletin of Economics and Statistics*, August, 173–195.

Lawrence, D. (1988). Globalizing the helicopter. *Vertilift*, September/October, p. 12.

Lawrence, P., and Lorsch, J. (1967). Differentiation and integration in complex organizations. *Administrative Science Quarterly*, 12, 1–47.

Lecraw, D. (1984). Bargaining power, ownership and profitability of transnational corporations in developing countries. *Journal of International Business*, Spring/Summer, 27–43.

Lehmann, D. (1979). *Market Research and Analysis*. Homewood, IL: Richard D. Irwin.

Lessard, D. (1983). Principles of international portfolio selection. In I. Giddy and A. George (Eds.), *International Finance Handbook*. New York: John Wiley.

Lessard, D. (1985). Transfer prices, taxes and financial markets: Implications of international financial transfers within the multinational corporation. In D. R. Lessard (Ed.), *International Financial Management: Theory and Application* (2nd ed.). New York: John Wiley & Sons.

Levitt, T. (1965). Exploit the product life cycle. *Harvard Business Review*, 45, 84–101.

Levitt, T. (1983). The globalization of markets. *Harvard Business Review*, 61, 92–102.

Leontiades, F. (1986). Going global: Global strategies vs. national strategies. *Long Range Planning*, 19, 96–104.

Lindert, P. H., and Kindleberger, C. P. (1982). *International Economics*, (7th ed.). Homewood, IL: Richard D. Irwin.

Lorange, P. (1989). Challenges to strategic planning process in multinational corporations. In A. Negandhi and A. Savara (Eds.), *International Strategic Management*. Lexington, MA: Lexington Books.

Lorange, P., Scott-Morton, M., and Ghoshal, S. (1986). *Strategic Control*. St. Paul, MN: West.

March, J., and Simon, H. (1958). *Organizations*. New York: Wiley.

Markides, C., and Berg, N. (1988). Manufacturing offshore is bad business. *Harvard Business Review*, Sept.-Oct., 113–120.

Mason, E. (1939). Price and production policies of large-scale enterprises. *American Economic Review*, March, 61–74.

Mayr, E. (1982). *The Growth of Biological Thought: Diversity, Evolution, and Inheritance*. Cambridge, MA: Harvard University Press.

McGee, J., and Thomas, H. (1988). Making sense of complex industries. In N. Hood and J. Vahlne (Eds.), *Strategies in Global Competition*. New York: Croom Helm.

McKelvey, B. (1975). Guidelines for empirical classification of organizations. *Administrative Sciences Quarterly*, 20, 509–525.

McKelvey, B. (1982). *Organizational Systematics: Taxonomy, Evolution, Classification*. Los Angeles: University of California Press.

McKinsey & Company. (1987). Winning in the world market. Study sponsored by the American Business Conference.

Miles, R., and Snow, C. (1978). *Organizational Strategy, Structure, and Process*. New York: McGraw-Hill.

Miles, R., and Snow, C. (1984). Fit, failure and the Hall of Fame. *California Management Review*, 26, 10–28.

Miller, D. (1986). Configurations of strategy and structure: Towards a synthesis. *Strategic Management Journal*, 7, 233–249.

Miller, D. (1987a). Strategy making and structure: Analysis and implications for performance. *Academy of Management Journal*, 30, 7–32.

Miller, D. (1987b). The structural and environmental correlates of business strategy. *Strategic Management Journal*, 8, 55–76.

Miller, D. (1988). Relating Porter's business strategies to environment and structure: Analysis and performance implications. *Academy of Management Journal*, 31, 280–308.

Miller, D., and Friesen, P. (1978). Archetypes of strategy formulation. *Management Science*, 24, 921–933.

Miller, D., and Toulouse, T. (1986). Strategy, structure, CEO personality and performance in small firms. *American Journal of Small Business*, Winter, 47–62.

Milligan, G. (1980). An examination of the effect of six types of error perturbation on fifteen clustering algorithms. *Psychometrika*, 45, 325–342.

Mintzberg, H. (1973). *The Nature of Managerial Work*. New York: Harper & Row.

Mintzberg, H. (1977). Policy as a field of management theory. *Academy of Management Review*, 2, 88–103.

Mintzberg, H. (1979a). Organizational power and goals: A skeletal theory. In D. Schendel and C. Hofer (Eds.), *Strategic Management*. Boston: Little, Brown.

Mintzberg, H. (1979b). *The Structuring of Organizations*. Englewood Cliffs, NJ: Prentice-Hall.

Mintzberg, H. (1987). Crafting strategy. *Harvard Business Review*, July/August, 66–75.

Montgomery, C. (1982). The measurement of firm diversification: Some new empirical evidence. *Academy of Management Journal*, 25, 299–307.

Moran, T. (1985). International political risk assessment, corporate planning, and strategies to offset political risk. In T. Moran (Ed.), *Multinational corporations: The Political Economy of Foreign Direct Investment*. Lexington, MA: Lexington Books.

Morrison, A. (1988). Dimensions of international business strategy: A conceptual examination. Paper presented as the Academy of International Business annual meeting, San Diego.

Morrison, A., and Roth, K. (1989). International business level strategy: The development of a holistic model. In A. Negandhi and A. Savara (Eds.), *International Strategic Management*. Lexington, MA: Lexington Press.

Morrison, D. (1967). Measurement problems in cluster analysis. *Management Science*, 13, B775–B780.

Murray, A. (1988). A contingency view of Porter's "Generic Strategies." *Academy of Management Review*, 13, 390–400.

Naumann-Etienne, R. (1974). A framework for financial decisions in multinational corporations: A summary of recent research. *Journal of Financial and Quantitative Analysis*, November, 859–874.

Neter, J., Wasserman, W., and Kutner, M. (1985). *Applied Linear Statistical Models* (2nd ed.). Homewood, IL: Richard D. Irwin.

Ohmae, K. (1982). *The Mind of the Strategist*. New York: McGraw-Hill.

Ohmae, K. (1985). *Triad Power: The Coming Shape of Global Competition*. New York: Free Press.

Ohmae, K. (1988). Getting back to strategy. *Harvard Business Review*, November/December 149–156.

Osborn, R., and Hunt, J. (1974). Environment and organization effectiveness. *Administrative Science Quarterly*, 19, 231–246.

Parsons, L. (1983). Information technology: A new competitive weapon. *Sloan Management Review*, 25, 3–14.

Perlmutter, H., and Heenan, D. (1986). Cooperate to compete globally. *Harvard Business Review*, March/April, 136–152.

Peters, T. (1986). Competition and compassion. *California Management Review*, Summer, 11–26.

Pfaffenberger, R., and Patterson, J. (1981). *Statistical Methods for Business and Economics*. Homewood, IL: Richard D. Irwin.

Pfeffer, J. (1987). Bringing the environment back in: The social context of business strategy. In D. Teece (Ed.), *The Competitive Challenge: Strategies for Industrial Innovation and Renewal*. Cambridge, MA: Ballinger Publishing.

Pitts, R., and Hopkins, D. (1982). Firm diversity: Conceptualization and measurement. *Academy of Management Review*, 74, 620–624.

Porter, M. E. (1980). *Competitive Strategy: Techniques for Analyzing Industries and Competitors*. New York: Free Press.

Porter, M. (1981). The contributions of industrial organization to strategic management. *Academy of Management Review*, 6, 609–620.

Porter, M. (1985). *Competitive Advantage*. New York: Free Press.

Porter, M. (1986a). Changing patterns of international competition. *California Management Review*, 28, 9–40.

Porter, M. (1986b). Competition in global industries: A conceptual framework. In M. Porter (Ed.), *Competition in Global Industries*. Boston: Harvard Business School.

Porter, M., and Fuller, M. (1986). Coalitions and global strategy. In M. Porter (Ed.), *Competition in Global Industries*. Boston: Harvard Business School.

Poynter, Thomas (1983). The corporate management of government intervention: A survival plan. Unpublished manuscript, University of Western Ontario.

Prahalad, C., and Bettis, R. (1986). The dominant logic: A new linkage between diversity and performance. *Strategic Management Journal*, 7, 485–501.

Prahalad, C., and Doz, Y. (1987). *The Multinational Mission: Balancing Local Demands and Global Vision*. New York: Free Press.

Prescott, J. (1983). Competitive environments, strategic types, and business performance: An empirical analysis. Ph.D. dissertation, Pennsylvania State University.

Punj, G., and Stewart, D. (1983). Cluster analysis in marketing research: Review and suggestions for application. *Journal of Marketing Research*, 20, 134–148.

Quelch, J., and Hoff, E. (1986). Customizing global marketing. *Harvard Business Review*, 64, 59–68.

Quinn, J. (1981). *Strategies for Change: Logical Incrementalism*. Homewood, IL: Richard D. Irwin.

Rabino, S. (1980). Tax incentives to exports: Some implications for policy makers. *Journal of International Business Studies*, Spring/Summer, 74–85.

Ragazzi, G. (1973). Theories of the determinants of direct foreign investment. *IMF Staff Papers*, July, 471–498.

Reich, R., and Mankin, E. (1986). Joint ventures with Japan give away our future. *Harvard Business Review*, March/April, 78–86.

Robinson, R. (1961). The challenge of the underdeveloped national market. *Journal of Marketing*, 25, 19–25.

Robinson, R., and Pearce, J. (1985). The structure of generic strategies and their impact on business-unit performance. *Academy of Management Proceedings*, San Diego, 35–39.

Robinson, R., and Pearce, J. (1988). Planned patterns of strategic behavior and their relationship to business-unit performance. *Strategic Management Journal*, 9, 43–60.

Root, F. (1987). *Entry Strategies for International Markets.* Lexington, MA: Lexington Books.

Roth, K. (1986). Strategic behavior and organizational performance: Construct and antecedent variable analysis in a causal model framework. Ph.D. dissertation, University of South Carolina.

Roth, K., and McDougall, P. (1986). An empirical comparison of domestic and international strategic behavior. Paper presented at the Academy of Management annual meeting, Chicago.

Rugman, A. (1979). *International Diversification and the Multinational Enterprise.* Lexington, MA: Lexington Books.

Rugman, A. (1985a). Internalization is still a general theory of foreign direct investment. *Weltwirtschaftliches Archiv*, September, 570–575.

Rugman, A. (1985b). New theories of the multinational enterprise: An assessment of international theory. Paper presented at the annual meeting of the Academy of International Business, New York.

Rugman, A., Lecraw, D., and Booth, L. (1985). *International Business: Firm and Environment.* New York: McGraw-Hill.

Rumelt, R. (1974). *Strategy, Structure and Economic Performance.* Boston: Harvard University Press.

Rutenberg, D. P. (1970). Maneuvering liquid assets in multinational companies: Formulation and deterministic solution procedures. *Management Science*, 16, B671–B684.

Rutenberg, D. (1981). Global product mandating. In K. C. Dhawan, H. Etemad, and R. Wright (Eds.), *International Business: A Canadian Perspective.* Don Mills, Ontario: Addison-Wesley.

Sarle, W. S. (1983). The cubic clustering criterion. SAS Technical Report A-108. Cary, NC: SAS Institute.

Sauer, W., Nighswonger, N., and Zaltman, G. (1983). Current issues in philosophy of science: Implications for the study of marketing. In S. Hunt (Ed.), *Marketing Theory: The Philosophy of Marketing Science.* Homewood, IL: Richard D. Irwin.

Schendel, D., and Hofer, C. (1979). *Strategic Management.* Boston: Little, Brown.

Schmenner, R. (1984). *Production/Operations Management: Concepts and Situations.* Chicago: SRA.

Schollhammer, H. (1973). Strategies and methodologies in international business and comparative management research. *Management International Review*, 13, 17–31.

Schonberger, R. (1982). *Japanese Manufacturing Technique.* New York: The Free Press.

Science Council of Canada. (1981). Multinationals and industrial strategy: The role of world product mandates. In K. Dhawan, H. Etemad, and R. Wright (Eds.), *International Business: A Canadian Perspective.* Don Mills, Ontario: Addison-Wesley.

Scott, B. (1973). The industrial state: Old myths and new realities. *Harvard Business Review*, March/April, 133–148.

Selznick, P. (1957). *Leadership in Administration.* White Plains, NY: Row, Peterson.

Sethi, S., and Luther, K. (1986). Political risk analysis and direct foreign investment: Some problems of definition and measurement. *California Management Review*, 28, 57–68.

Shapiro, A. (1978). Capital budgeting for the multinational corporation. *Financial Management*, Spring, 7–16.

Simon, J. (1982). Political risk assessment: Past trends and future prospects. *Columbia Journal of World Business*, 17, 62–71.

Singer, D. (1961). The level of analysis problem in international relations. *World Politics*, 14, 77–92.

Skinner, W. (1985). *Manufacturing: The Formidable Competitive Weapon*. New York: John Wiley.

Smith, K., and Grimm, C. (1987). Environmental variation, strategic change and firm performance: A study of railroad deregulation. *Strategic Management Journal*, 8, 363–376.

Sneath, P., and Sokal, R. (1973). *Numerical Taxonomy: The Principals and Practice of Numerical Classification*. San Francisco: W. H. Freeman.

Snow, C., and Hambrick, D. (1980). Measuring organizational strategies: Some theoretical and methodological problems. *Academy of Management Review*, 5, 527–538.

Solnik, B. (1974). Why not diversify internationally rather than domestically? *Financial Analysts Journal*, July/August, 48–54.

Spender, J. (1979). Theory building and theory testing in strategic management: Commentary. In D. Schendel and C. Hofer (Eds.), *Strategic Management: A New View of Business Policy and Planning*. Boston: Little, Brown.

Srinivasan, V., and Kim, Y. (1986). Payments netting in international cash management: A network optimization approach. *Journal of International Business Studies*, 17, 1–20.

Steiner, G. (1979). Contingency theories of strategic management. In D. Schendel and C. Hofer (Eds.), *Strategic Management: A New View of Business Policy and Planning*. Boston: Little, Brown.

Stewart, D. (1981). The application and misapplication of factor analysis in marketing research. *Journal of Marketing Research*, 18, 51–62.

Stone, N. (1989). The globalization of Europe: An interview with Wisse Dekker. *Harvard Business Review*, May/June, 90–95.

Stopford, J., and Wells, L. (1972). *Managing the Multinational Enterprise*. New York: Basic Books.

Takeuchi, H., and Nonaka, I. (1986). The new product development game. *Harvard Business Review*, January/February, 137–146.

Takeuchi, H., and Porter, M. (1986). Three roles of marketing in global strategy. In M. Porter (Ed.), *Competition in Global Industries*. Boston: Harvard Business School.

Teece, D. (1986). Transactions cost economics and the multinational enterprise. *Journal of Economic Behavior and Organization*, 7, 21–45.

Thompson, J. (1967). *Organizations in Action*. New York: McGraw-Hill.

Tilles, S. (1963). How to evaluate a corporate strategy. Harvard Business Review, July/August, 111–121.

Tilles, S. (1966). Strategies for allocating funds. *Harvard Business Review*, 44, 72–80.

Tomlinson, J. (1970). *The Joint Venture Process in International Business: India and Pakistan*. Cambridge, MA: MIT Press.

Tregoe, B., and Zimmerman, J. (1980). *Top Management: What It Is and How to Make It Work*. New York: Simon and Schuster.

Uterback, J., and Abernathy, W. (1975). A dynamic model of process and product innovation. *OMEGA*, 3, 639–656.

Vancil, R. (1976). Strategy formulation in complex organizations. *Sloan Management Review*, 17, 1–18.

Vancil, R., and Lorange, P. (1975). Strategic planning in diversified organizations. *Harvard Business Review*, 53, 81–90.

Venkatraman, N., and Camillus, J. (1984). Exploring the concept of "fit" in strategic management. *Academy of Management Review*, 9, 513–525.

Venkatraman, N., and Grant, J. (1986). Construct measurement in organizational strategy research: A critique and proposal. *Academy of Management Review*, 11, 71–87.

Vernon, R. (1966). International investment and international trade in the product cycle. *Quarterly Journal of Economics*, 80, 190–207.

Vernon, R. (1971). *Sovereignty at Bay*. New York: Basic Books.

Vernon, R. (1979). The product cycle hypothesis in a new international environment. *Oxford Bulletin of Economics and Statistics*, 41, 255–267.

Wallace, W. (1971). *The Logic of Science in Sociology*. New York: Aldine Publishing.

Weick, K. (1979). *The Social Psychology of Organizing*. New York: Random House.

White, R. (1986). Generic Business Strategies, organizational context and performance: An empirical investigation. *Strategic Management Journal*, 7, 217–231.

White, R., and Poynter, T. (1984). Strategies for foreign-owned subsidiaries in Canada. *Business Quarterly*, Summer, 59–69.

Williamson, O. (1975). *Markets and Hierarchies: Analysis and Antitrust Implications*. New York: Free Press.

Wissema, J., Van der Pol, J., and Messer, H. (1980). Strategic management archetypes. *Strategic Management Journal*, 1, 37–47.

Wolf, A. (1926). *Essentials of Scientific Method*. New York: Macmillan.

Woo, C., and Cool, K. (1983). Porter's (1980) generic competitive strategies: A test of performance and functional strategy attributes. Working paper, Purdue University.

Wrigley, L. (1970). Divisional autonomy and diversification. Ph.D. dissertation, Harvard Business School.

Yip, G. (1982a). *Barriers to Entry*. Lexington, MA: Lexington Books.

Yip, G. (1982b). Gateways to entry. *Harvard Business Review*, September/October, 85–92.

Yoshino, M. (1986). Global competition in a salient industry: The case of civil aircraft. In M. Porter (Ed.), *Competition in Global Industries*. Boston: Harvard Business School.

Zeithaml, C., and Fry, L. (1984). Contextual and strategic differences among mature businesses in four dynamic performance situations. *Academy of Management Journal*, 27, 841–860.

INDEX

ABOUT THE AUTHOR

ALLEN J. MORRISON is Assistant Professor of Business Policy and International Business at the Western Ontario School of Business Administration at the University of Western Ontario. He won the 1989 Barry M. Richmond award for best dissertation in international business at the Academy of Management. Professor Morrison has written and lectured extensively on competition in global industries and the strategic management of multinational corporations.